Steva
713-9

dry

ANSWERS
For College Students

Blessings!
Steve Williamson
Psalm 32:8

By
STEVAN F. WILLIAMSON

TABLE OF CONTENTS

ACKNOWLEDGEMENTS

I'd like to thank Mrs. Johnnye Gautier, my high school English teacher, who encouraged my early attempts at writing. Your positive feedback and friendly smile helped me believe in myself. Now all these years later, you are still reaching students through the love of writing you instilled in me. Thanks, Mrs. G.

Thanks to my son Jonathan and Daughter-in-Love Liza for reviewing this book and making sure my ideas resonated with young adults. Your lives serve as a witness to others of how God will walk beside you through college and beyond.

Thanks to my daughters Lauren and Madelyn for being my inspiration for this book. Remember, God will always be there for you and He has an answer for whatever you may face in life. Thanks for loving me and always making me proud.

Thanks to my wonderful wife, Robin, who supported, encouraged, and gently nudged me forward to complete this assignment. Next to my salvation, marrying you is still the best decision I ever made.

PREFACE

When my son started his journey into college, I prayed for his safety, his success, and his future. During his first year, he learned valuable lessons about life and living on his own. The experience reminded me of my own days as a college student. I remember wonderful fun-filled days without a care in the world except making it to class on time. I met many new friends and explored my newly found independence. I also remember another side that sometimes dealt with loneliness, temptation, and a fear of my future.

When my daughter started college, I felt a new set of emotions. I worried about her safety. Who would watch over her and protect her? I thought about boys. Who would be there to chaperone? Then I realized she would face many of these things on her own. The transition into college is the beginning of an independent life. While it presents concerns for me as a parent, it provides many new challenges for the student.

This book was written to help college students in this exciting time of transition into adulthood. As you begin your journey towards the future, don't forget to include

God in your life. He will truly light your path and give you the direction you need to succeed. When you take a wrong turn, or get off God's path, He will gently lead you back in the right direction.

I hope you find the advice in this book helpful, comforting, and the encouragement you need to keep moving forward.

God Bless You,

Stevan F. Williamson

INTRODUCTION

We all struggle on this journey through life. Along the way, we go through different phases: Childhood, Teenage, Young Adult, Middle Age, and Old Age. However, the transition you make during your college years is unique. During these years, you are often alone for the first time. You are making choices about your future. You are meeting many new people and being exposed to many new things. This can be a very exciting time but also be a bit overwhelming.

When those times come (and they will come) when you feel nervous or confused, there is no better remedy than reading God's Word. The Bible was created as a guidebook for you to go through life. Nothing builds your faith like reading God's Word. The Bible says the Scripture is alive.

For the word of God is alive and powerful. It is sharper than the sharpest two-edged sword, cutting between soul and spirit, between joint and marrow. It exposes our innermost thoughts and desires. (Hebrews 4:12)

All Scripture is inspired by God and is useful to teach us what is true and to make us realize what is wrong in our lives. It corrects us when we are wrong and teaches us to do what is right. God uses it to prepare and equip his people to do every good work. (2 Timothy 3:16-17)

Whenever you are dealing with an issue, the Bible should always be the first place to look for answers. If you're not sure how to find the right Scripture, pick up this book and check the table of contents. Each chapter addresses a common issue you will face in your college years. Read the commentary under each topic but more importantly check out the Scriptures. They will bring joy, hope, and healing to you whatever the situation. I've included a few key Scriptures in every chapter and *many more* in the Appendix. If you aren't sure how to pray, I've included some prayers as well. Think of this an important textbook for your college life. Carry it in your backpack, handbag, or car so it will be available when you need it. College is an amazing journey. Keep God close by.

Chapter 1

ANGER

S chool can be so frustrating! You want to get through this class and never think about it again. What's with that professor? Doesn't he know you are taking other classes besides his? The homework load is crazy! Maybe you've had a falling out with your boyfriend or girlfriend because they said or did something that made you so mad! You're thinking, "I really don't need this drama right now."

You want to move on, but you are frustrated by a person or situation. What do you do? It really boils down to two choices. Either lash out, (which might feel good briefly but will ultimately cause more damage), or just let it go and move past the anger. I know that it's easier said than done. The problem is anger has a way of festering up inside of you. It will occupy your mind so you have difficulty studying, or even sleeping. It can churn inside your stomach and heart to the point of even making you physically ill.

God understands your anger. He created you, and gave you all the emotions you feel inside... love, kindness, joy, sadness, and even anger. However, like all things with God,

He wants you to remain in control. He understands that you get angry from time to time. Everyone has a bad day. The Scriptures say that when you do get angry, don't let it cause you to sin. God doesn't want to see this anger develop into a pattern in your life. People who can't control their anger often find themselves in even more difficult situations. Anger pushes away friends and hurts the people you love. On the extreme side, you'll find that prison is filled with individuals who couldn't control their anger and lashed out at someone or something.

God's Word is full of sound advice about anger. Most of it boils down to this. Be slow to anger. I've heard people say, "I can't help it. That's just how I am." Well, it may be who you are now, but it isn't how you were created. God didn't form you as a child full of anger and spite. Your short temper and impatience is something you've developed over a lifetime of challenges and disappointments.

God wants you to be full of the Spirit. The Holy Spirit wants to help produce this kind of fruit in your life: love, joy, peace, patience, kindness, goodness, faithfulness, gentleness, and self-control. The choice is yours. You can be stubborn and do what your flesh tells you, or you can opt to follow God's direction for your life. Remember, you shouldn't let outside circumstances determine how you react to the world. If it helps, count to ten before you speak. Study the Scriptures below and get them into your heart and mind. God is clear on how He feels about anger and the impact it has on you and those around you.

Say this prayer...

God, help me to control my anger. I try to be patient, but sometimes I get so frustrated that it just comes out. Forgive me for my anger and help me to be more self-controlled. I want to be a picture of You to other people. I want to reflect Your joy and kindness Lord. I release this anger to You and ask You to heal my heart and mind from any hurt, or injustice in my past that may be lingering inside of me. Replace my anger with joy and peace. I ask this in Jesus' Name. Amen.

What does the Bible tell us?

...You must all be quick to listen, slow to speak, and slow to get angry. Human anger does not produce the righteousness God desires. (James 1:19-20)

A fool is quick-tempered, but a wise person stays calm when insulted. (Proverbs 12:16)

Short-tempered people do foolish things... (Proverbs 14:17)

People with understanding control their anger; a hot temper shows great foolishness. (Proverbs 14:29)

Fools vent their anger, but the wise quietly hold it back. (Proverbs 29:11)

Control your temper, for anger labels you a fool. (Ecclesiastes 7:9)

And "don't sin by letting anger control you." Don't let the sun go down while you are still angry, for anger gives a foothold to the devil. (Ephesians 4:26-27)

Chapter 2

ANXIETY & STRESS

I am so stressed! You hear this often these days. The increasing pressures that society places on us, and we place on ourselves can be overwhelming. You can be stressed about almost anything! You stress about your grades, where to live, how to pay your rent, what to wear, what *not* to wear, dating, losing weight, graduation, finding a job, and moving apartments to name a few.

How do you manage all this stress? First, you need to understand the root of it all. It may surprise you that it is simply... Fear. This can't be true. You're not afraid of anything right? Well, let's examine your stress. Why are you so stressed about this particular thing? If you search inside yourself, you are probably afraid something bad is going to happen. You're afraid you will flunk the upcoming test. You're afraid you won't have enough money to pay your rent. You're afraid the person you are interested in won't ask you out. You're afraid of gaining weight. All these situations are rooted in fear.

In fact, stress and anxiety are just fancy words for fear. No, it's not the same kind of fear as when you are robbed, or watch a scary movie. It is a milder form that simply makes you "uncomfortable." An analogy would be a hot coal versus a raging fire. Both are hot, but one is just simmering beneath the surface. This is why stress goes untreated for so long. It isn't always a bold, aggressive attack, but a subtle consistent attack. We'll explore this more in the chapter on fear.

Here's the good news. No matter what you call it, the treatment is the same. Go to the Bible. There are many Scriptures about how to conquer anxiety. Whether your stress is related to your school, finances, relationships, or your future, the Bible provides answers and reassurances to help relieve your stress. God says to *"give all your worries and cares to God, because He cares for about you."* Isn't it great to know you have a caring God who wants the best for your life? There's no reason for you to worry. Let him take care of you and your situation. Examine the Scriptures below to learn what God says about anxiety, worry, and stress.

Say this prayer...

God, please help me with this anxiety. Help me avoid being stressed or anxious about things. I know You want the best for me, but sometimes I'm afraid. Help me not be afraid and simply trust in you. I am so tense and nervous about things. Help me to relax. I ask You to replace my anxiety with peace, and my stress with the comfort of your Holy Spirit. I ask this in Jesus' Name. Amen.

What does the Bible tell us?

Give all your worries and cares to God, for he cares about you. (1 Peter 5:7)

Give your burdens to the Lord, and he will take care of you. He will not permit the godly to slip and fall. (Psalm 55:22)

Don't worry about anything; instead, pray about everything. Tell God what you need, and thank him for all he has done. Then you will experience God's peace, which exceeds anything we can under-stand. His peace will guard your hearts and minds as you live in Christ Jesus. (Philippians 4:6-7)

And this same God who takes care of me will supply all your needs from his glorious riches, which have been given to us in Christ Jesus. (Philippians 4:19)

And we know that God causes everything to work together for the good of those who love God... (Romans 8:28)

Worry weighs a person down; an encouraging word cheers a person up. (Proverbs 12:25)

Can all your worries add a single moment to your life? And if worry can't accomplish a little thing like that, what's the use of worrying over bigger things? (Luke 12:25-26)

Chapter 3

DATING

A nother interesting experience in college is dating. You leave behind a high school where you know most people and arrive at college where you don't know anyone. The whole thing is a bit awkward because your classmates are mostly strangers. On the other hand, it can be exciting because you are meeting so many new people. Then nature takes its course and you finally meet someone you are interested in dating. You may try a little small talk like "Where are you from?" or "What's your major?" That's all fine when you are becoming acquainted, but at some point you need to focus on what's most important in your relationship.

The Bible doesn't talk much about "dating" because the concept wasn't common back then. It does talk a great deal about courtship, relationships, and of course, love. Most people think of dating as going to dinner or catching a movie. Some dates are this simple, but eventually you feel a connection with someone. You wonder if this could lead to something more serious. Then, dating becomes like an extended interview. You are trying to decide if you want to be in a relationship. I'm not saying every date is leading toward marriage. I'm just saying relationships are a part of life. You want someone who understands your dreams, has the same sense of humor, likes the same movies, or whatever. Most of us are looking for someone with common interests and with whom we enjoy spending time.

Let's dig a bit deeper. If you are looking for a relationship, you definitely want someone compatible, but you are also looking for someone whose personality complements yours. For example, you may be a detailed person and they are a big picture person. You are cautious, and they are more spontaneous. Sometimes these differences work well together. This is why they say, "Opposites attract." My wife and I each have areas where one is stronger or weaker. Those are the areas where we support each other. I step in when she is struggling, and vice versa. We're a team after the same goals.

If you are thinking about a longer-term relationship, please consider this. You want someone who has a relationship with Christ. The Bible clearly states that Christians shouldn't be permanently connected (married) to someone who doesn't believe in Christ. Remember, going to church doesn't make you a Christian. This only happens by making a decision to accept Jesus as your Savior.

Don't be fooled by individuals who call themselves "spiritual." This may have nothing to do with God. There are many spirits in the world, but only one Holy Spirit. When a believer is paired with a non-believer, they create a dysfunctional team. For marriage to succeed, you need to be a team with common goals and a common belief. Often we pursue physical attraction and overlook the spiritual part of the relationship. If you are considering a more serious relationship with an individual, you want to be aligned in terms of your beliefs. During this dating season, explore who they are and what they believe.

God's word is also clear about some other elements of your relationships: Avoid sex before marriage, guard your heart, and treat one another with respect. It may sound old fashioned, but God hasn't changed these rules in a very long time. Like any good Father, He wants the right companion for His child. He sees the marriage statistics, and the lack of commitment in the world today. He still believes in one spouse for life. That means picking the right one. Before you even start the dating scene, have a chat with your heavenly Father. He knows the perfect person for you.

Say this prayer...

(If you are looking for someone)
Lord, help me find the right person for me. I want to meet someone who loves You God, and therefore understands love because You are the Father of love. I want someone who will love me with all of their heart. I want someone with whom I can truly bond. I need someone I can take care of and will take care of me. I'm looking for someone who will stay beside me on this journey of life. Help me to stay away from the wrong choices and keep me from temptations. I know the right one is out there for me. Help me find that person. I ask this in Jesus' Name. Amen.

(If you are getting serious with someone)

Lord, I think this is the right person for me. If we are meant to be together, give me a peace that this is the right person for this next step of commitment. I enjoy our time together, and I have strong feelings for them. I think they feel the same, but I want Your blessing. I know any successful relationship is built on love and needs to be centered on You... the Father of love. Help us to keep our physical relationship pure. Keep us out of intimate situations that would tempt us to sin. Help us to grow closer to You as we grow closer to each other. I ask this in Jesus' Name. Amen.

What does the Bible tell us?

Guard your heart above all else, for it determines the course of your life. (Proverbs 4:23)

Don't team up with those who are unbelievers. How can righteousness be a partner with wickedness? How can light live with darkness? What harmony can there be between Christ and the devil? How can a believer be a partner with an unbeliever? (2 Corinthians 6:14-15)

Love is patient and kind. Love is not jealous or boastful or proud or rude. Love does not demand its own way. Love is not irritable, and it keeps no record of when it has been wronged. It is never glad about injustice but rejoices whenever the truth wins out. Love never gives up, never loses faith, is always hopeful, and endures through every circumstance. (1 Corinthians 13:4-7)

Run from anything that stimulates youthful lusts. Instead, pursue righteous living, faithfulness, love, and peace. Enjoy the companionship of those who call on the Lord with pure hearts. (2 Timothy 2:22)

... treat younger women with all purity as you would your own sisters. (1 Timothy 5:2)

God's will is for you to be holy, so stay away from all sexual sin. Then each of you will control his own body and live in holiness and honor—not in lustful passion like the pagans who do not know God and his ways. (1 Thessalonians 4:3-5)

Don't let anyone think less of you because you are young. Be an example to all believers in what you say, in the way you live, in your love, your faith, and your purity. (1 Timothy 4:12)

Chapter 4

DECISIONS

The transition from high school to college can be a confusing journey. You are bombarded with so many decisions! You have to decide where to go to college. Should you go where your friends are going? Should you go where your heart is telling you? Should you simply go to the place that is closest to home or offers a scholarship? How do you decide on a major? What classes should you take? Will this decision affect the rest of your life? Should you live, on-campus or off-campus? There are so many new acronyms and your classes are in so many buildings. A lot of pressure can come from these decisions and it can become overwhelming.

While college can be full of decisions, it is also the stepping-stone into your adult life. Without your parents around, you may be forced to make independent decisions for the first time. This can feel liberating, but it can also be scary. Then, as you approach graduation, more issues confront you like finding a job, moving to another city, and many other changes. As you face each of these dilemmas, you want to make the right decision. You want make smart decisions to prepare you for what comes next.

Here's the good news. You have the ultimate Advisor. You can simply ask the Holy Spirit for direction. The Bible calls Him your Comforter, and Counselor. Do you remember your high school counselor? Their job was to answer questions, give you advice, and help you get started in the right direction. Imagine what it would be like to get the advice of God's own Spirit! He knows your future. He knows which direction will be successful, and He knows the desires of your heart.

You can ask the Holy Spirit for advice on the smallest detail or the most difficult decision. God sent the Holy Spirit to be your own private counselor. His job is to point you in the right direction for success and to keep you out of trouble. Like any good counselor, He is extremely knowledgeable about the options available. His specialty is leading others to success, and He has a vast amount of experience.

Even if you aren't sure what you want out of life, God still has a plan for you. The Scriptures tell us He has a plan for your life. If you ask God to be a part of it, He will make sure your plans succeed. His plans will always lead to good things, and He will provide hope for your future. As you walk into the unknown, the Bible says He will be a light to show you the way through the darkness.

Say this prayer...

Holy Spirit, thank You for watching over me. I know You are here to help me and I need Your help with some decisions. Every day I face new challenges and sometimes I get stuck in indecision. Give me wisdom to make the right choices. Give me direction and guidance for my future. Show me the correct path forward for my life. I'm not sure which way to go and I'm afraid of making the wrong decision. Give me guidance and your supernatural peace to know things will be OK. Wrap your arms around me and give me comfort, wisdom, and divine counseling on what to do in every situation. I ask this in Jesus' Name. Amen.

What does the Bible tell us?

Trust in the Lord with all your heart; do not depend on your own understanding. Seek his will in all you do, and he will show you which path to take. (Proverbs 3:5-6)

Look straight ahead, and fix your eyes on what lies before you. Mark out a straight path for your feet; stay on the safe path. Don't get sidetracked; keep your feet from following evil. (Proverbs 4:25-27)

Do not be afraid or discouraged, for the Lord will personally go ahead of you. He will be with you; he will neither fail you nor abandon you." (Deuteronomy 31:8)

If you need wisdom, ask our generous God, and he will give it to you. He will not rebuke you for asking. (James 1:5)

Commit your actions to the Lord, and your plans will succeed. (Proverbs 16:3)

For I know the plans I have for you," says the Lord. "They are plans for good and not for disaster, to give you a future and a hope. (Jeremiah 29:11)

Your word is a lamp to guide my feet and a light for my path. (Psalm 119:105)

Chapter 5

DEPRESSION

Do you ever get overwhelmed by the pressures of life? You have to deal with so many school issues like homework, grades, and deciding what to take next semester. Then you worry about other things like finances, losing weight, and dating. Your mind starts to wonder about everything. Why does everything I eat go to my stomach or my thighs? Why do all my friends have a boyfriend, but not me? Why did I choose this major? What was I thinking? We all have times like this. Life has a way of stacking things on your shoulders until you can feel overwhelmed. When you can't see a way out, it's easy to get depressed.

Depression comes in different levels and affects individuals differently. You may just feel a little sad or melancholy. You want to watch sad movies and eat ice cream. We all have times when we feel a bit "down." For others, depression is more severe. You don't have the energy to get out of bed. You withdraw from others. Depression makes you want to stay in bed and sleep. You would rather spend time in darkness than the light. This is true both physically and spiritually. For some, depression can become a serious and crippling condition. What does the Bible say about depression?

The Bible talks about having a sad heart. It even talks about having a broken heart and having your spirit crushed. God knows how you feel. There is nothing is new to Him. He understands sadness and hopelessness. He understands it when you have lost the desire to keep moving forward.

Here's the good news. God has a solution to your depression. He can provide you encouragement, joy, strength, confidence. He can supply whatever you need to push through the situation. You are one of God's children and He will never leave you or forsake you. He is always there to help you out of your depression. Just ask Him!

When you were a child, you may have been nervous about meeting new people or trying new things. Maybe it was your first rollercoaster, or first time riding a pony. You would look up into your Father's eyes to see what he thought. You were looking for him to say, "It's OK... you'll be fine." "I'm right behind you, you can do it!"

Nothing has changed really. You are just a little taller. You still want your Father's protection and encouragement. Just look up to God. He is your heavenly Father and you are His child. Instead of looking at your circumstances, which seem scary and insurmountable, fix your eyes on God. He is there for you. Maybe your earthly father wasn't around much. Your childhood may have left you with a certain level of insecurity. There was no one to encourage and console you. That's where God is different. God is always with you. He will never abandon you. He is standing right there beside you. Even now as you read this book.

God's Word encourages us to come out of the darkness and into the light! Before you were born, God knew you would go through this difficult time. The Scriptures offer some encouraging words to help you through this. Don't let the devil fool you into thinking this is only happening to you. Everyone deals with this from time to time. Read the Scriptures below and let God's Word strengthen and encourage you. If you read closely, you'll see He is telling you, "You can do it!"

Say this prayer...

Father, I feel so discouraged. I can't seem to find my way out of this depression. Please hear my prayers Lord. I'm weak. I'm almost too tired to pray. Pull me out of this depression. Help me pick up the pieces of my life and live again. Heal me Lord... mentally, physically, and emotionally. I know You want the best for me. Show me Your love and help me to love myself. Give me peace, happiness, and a positive outlook on my life. Holy Spirit... the Bible says You are the Comforter. Comfort me now... help me to feel Your love. Restore my confidence and my joy. I want to live a full life. I know You want me to have a happy life. Take me out of the darkness and into Your light. I ask this in Jesus' Name. Amen.

What does the Bible tell us?

The Lord hears his people when they call to him for help. He rescues them from all their troubles. The Lord is close to the brokenhearted; he rescues those whose spirits are crushed. The righteous person faces many troubles, but the Lord comes to the rescue each time. (Psalm 34:17-19)

He heals the brokenhearted and bandages their wounds. (Psalm 147:3)

Give your burdens to the Lord, and he will take care of you. He will not permit the godly to slip and fall. (Psalm 55:22)

He lifted me out of the pit of despair, out of the mud and the mire. He set my feet on solid ground and steadied me as I walked along. (Psalm 40:2)

But in my distress I cried out to the Lord; yes, I prayed to my God for help. He heard me from his sanctuary; my cry to him reached his ears. (Psalm 18:6)

He will once again fill your mouth with laughter and your lips with shouts of joy. (Job 8:21)

For I know the plans I have for you," says the Lord. "They are plans for good and not for disaster, to give you a future and a hope. (Jeremiah 29:11)

Chapter 6

DRINKING

In today's culture, alcohol flows freely and drinking is considered socially acceptable for many. Some of you were introduced to alcohol in high school or even younger. You may have seen your parents drink and just accepted it as a way of life. Regardless of what you have seen or experienced in this area, you will need to make a personal decision about drinking alcoholic beverages. This isn't just about underage drinking (which is illegal); it's about personal choices you have to make as an adult. You want those choices to be biblically based.

What does the Bible say about drinking alcohol? It might surprise you that no Scripture specifically says you can't drink. However, there are *many* Scriptures telling you not to get *drunk*. God is not interested in a debate about wine versus beer. He simply wants you to understand the effects of drinking. God wants to protect you. He wants to keep you safe, and help you make wise decisions.

Since the Scriptures seem to focus on getting drunk, let's first examine the legal view of intoxication. Different countries have specific limits deemed as "driving under the influence" or "driving while intoxicated." This is based on your blood/alcohol concentration. In the United States, .08 percent blood alcohol concentration is the legal limit when driving. Notice this is less than one tenth of a percent! It really doesn't take much alcohol to affect you. That's why you should never drink and drive, no matter how much you've consumed.

Here is the mystery question. Can you drink and not get drunk? Some people would say, "Sure…if you just keep it to one or two drinks." Others would say that intoxication really begins with the first drink. The truth is that drinking affects everyone differently. Even a small amount of alcohol can affect you, and there's no simple way to tell whether you're within the legal limit. Alcohol's effect on your body depends on multiple factors including: your age, your weight, your gender, whether you've eaten, or even how tired you are. It also depends on the type of alcohol you're drinking.

Adults often talk about having a drink to relax. This sounds harmless, but alcohol is metabolized extremely quickly by the body. About 20 percent is absorbed directly through an empty stomach and can reach the brain within one minute. Your mind is being affected much faster than you think. Even with one drink, your thinking can be impaired. Often your first drink leads to another and another. You may not plan to get intoxicated, but statistics show this is often the result with young adults.

The real question is this. How do you know if you are you drunk? If the police pull you over, they will do a breathalyzer test and will tell you whether you are past the "legal" limit. Well, most of us don't own a breathalyzer. You don't really know what your blood alcohol content is. The experts tell us *any* amount of alcohol affects your judgment and your ability to drive safely. You may not notice the effects, but even a small amount of alcohol can reduce your co-ordination. It can slow down your reaction time, affect your vision, affect how you judge speed and distance, and make you drowsy. If you're going to drink, plan beforehand how you'll get home without driving.

Let's be clear. God's concern with drunkenness isn't only about driving. The Scriptures were written long before automobiles. God's not even focused strictly on the legality of it all. He gave us His instructions long before there were laws about this. God is concerned about your "behavior," and how alcohol can affect you.

Alcohol affects your mind and body. Too much alcohol can give you a distorted version of reality. It not only slows down your reflexes and your reaction time, but it can also make you more likely to take risks. This can create dangerous situations for you and those around you. When you are under the influence, you may try something dangerous because your view of reality is blurred. You aren't as strong, fast, funny, or invulnerable as the alcohol would make you think. And it lingers. There's really no quick way of sobering up. Drinking coffee or taking a cold shower might help wake you up, but it doesn't lessen the amount of alcohol in your bloodstream.

Drinking also loosens your inhibitions, and often reduces your self-control. For some, having too much to drink manifests as anger, and a releasing of pent up frustrations. This sounds harmless until you to say or do something harmful to others. Alcohol has sparked many fights and physical confrontations. There's a reason we have terms like "bar fight."

Statistics also show that excessive drinking can cause a loosening of moral values. Intoxication can place you in an unintended intimate situation with someone. Is one night of partying worth the shame and guilt of an unintended sexual encounter? Regrettably, there are also people who prey on individuals who are impaired by alcohol. They take advantage of you when your guard is down. Don't let excessive drinking leave you in a vulnerable condition.

People say things like: "What's the big deal?", "I'm not hurting anyone.", "I'm just having fun." Tell that to a family who has lost a loved one because you decided to drive drunk. Tell that to your parents when they come to bail you out of jail. Every week we hear on the news that something awful has happened to a young adult. All their friends and family are left to pick up the pieces of their life. Don't let this happen to you.

There's no need to get into a debate about the right or wrong of drinking. You simply have to make a choice. Choose wisely. Avoid drinking to excess. For some of you, this means never taking that first drink. Below are a few Scriptures that show how God feels about this subject. He offers more direct advice than you might think.

Say this prayer...

Lord, help me to make smart choices. As I follow your Word, I know it will lead me in the right direction. Help me to follow your instructions and avoid getting drunk. I won't let society, my friends, or the desire to be popular influence me. Help me to follow your guidance and be a proper role model as one of your followers. If I'm going to be under the influence, I want it to be Your influence. Free me from any addictions, and temptations. Forgive me when I've messed up, and help me to start again and stand strong. I ask this in Jesus' Name. Amen.

What does the Bible tell us?

Don't be drunk with wine, because that will ruin your life. Instead, be filled with the Holy Spirit (Ephesians 5:18)

Night is the time when people sleep and drinkers get drunk. But let us who live in the light be clearheaded... (1 Thessalonians 5:7-8)

What sorrow for those who get up early in the morning looking for a drink of alcohol and spend long evenings drinking wine to make themselves flaming drunk. (Isaiah 5:11)

What sorrow for those who are heroes at drinking wine and boast about all the alcohol they can hold. (Isaiah 5:22)

Watch out! Don't let your hearts be dulled by carousing and drunkenness... (Luke 21:34)

My child, listen and be wise: Keep your heart on the right course. Do not carouse with drunkards... (Proverbs 23:19-20)

You say, "I am allowed to do anything"—but not everything is good for you. And even though "I am allowed to do anything," I must not become a slave to anything. (1 Corinthians 6:12)

Chapter 7

DRUGS

Life is about making smart choices. When it comes to drugs, statistics show some clearly documented patterns. I'll keep it simple by just saying this: When you do drugs, bad things happen. Just watch the news and you'll see evidence that illegal drugs can lead to extremely dangerous situations.

Don't be lured by the "experience" or "social" aspects of drugs, or be foolish enough to be "dared" into trying drugs. The fact is drugs affect your brain. It's that simple. Drugs are designed to be "mind altering." I know people try to make it sound "cool." You can even feel pressured because "everyone" is doing it. Here is the truth. Nothing good comes from getting high. Smoking used to be cool too, but now we know it contributes to lung cancer. Frankly, ingesting anything harmful into your body just to look cool is pretty dumb.

Some people use drugs to escape. You want to get away from your problems and the pressures of life. You want to forget about what's worrying you. You want to escape your situation by using some mind-altering substances. Unfortunately, it is a temporary escape. After you come down from the drug, your problems are still there.

Instead of turning to drugs, maybe it's time for you to look inward. Find out what's causing your feelings. What are you trying to escape? Talk to God and tell Him what's bothering you. Maybe the issue you are dealing with is addressed in another chapter of this book. Read those chapters and see what God has to say about your situation. God can turn your life around in a heartbeat. He can heal you and restore your hope. Never be ashamed to seek professional help if you need it.

As society continues to loosen its moral grip, certain drugs like marijuana are becoming legal. It is considered a minor drug compared to the harder stuff like cocaine, crack, heroin, ecstasy, etc. However, even these minor drugs can have devastating consequences because they affect your mind and give you a distorted version of reality. The temporary escape from reality is not worth the consequences. Being "cool" isn't worth killing your brain cells. This is college! You need those brain cells!

Even taking drugs once can lead to unfortunate circumstances. Those who become addicted enter a world that is worse than they could ever imagine. Young adults who were once innocent have stolen things, hurt loved ones, and even sold their own bodies to get their next "fix." You think it won't happen to you. Guess what? Nobody ever plans to become addicted. You may think of drug addicts as the dregs of society but many of them were once just like you. They just took a terrible fall down the wrong road. Their parents and friends suffer along with them. Don't be naïve. You are smart! You've seen on TV what drugs can do to a person. It doesn't just happen to the weak. The best way to avoid addiction is to stay away from illegal drugs. It seems simple, but abstinence really is the best choice.

Drugs, as we know them today, weren't around in the Bible days. No Scriptures speak directly to a particular drug, but God isn't focused on a particular drug or drink. He is interested in your behavior. God is concerned about anything that alters your mind to the point where you are making poor decisions. The Scriptures from the chapter on drinking can also be applied to getting high. Since the drugs we're talking about are typically illegal, we must also obey the laws of the land.

God has given you His Spirit to dwell inside of you. Caring for your body is not just a physical thing but also a spiritual thing. Polluting or harming your body is like desecrating the temple of God. Here is a final thought to consider. The Bible tells us the devil is constantly searching for someone who is weak enough for him to devour. Predators look for prey that is weak, hurt, or has wandered away from the safety of their family. When you take drugs, you are making a conscious decision to separate yourself from the family of God because you are going against His will. Because you are ingesting something that alters your mind, you aren't alert enough to see the attack of the devil coming. Don't put yourself in that place. Stay close to God. Follow His voice. In addition to the Scriptures in the previous chapter, below are a few more Scriptures to show how God feels about this subject.

Say this prayer...

(If you are tempted...)
Lord, I'm trying to stay away from drugs, but some of the people I hang around with keep pressuring me to try them. I see people experimenting with drugs at parties and they

seem to be having a good time. I'm tempted to try something just to know how it feels. I know it isn't right, but I feel drawn toward it. Is it my curiosity? Is it the devil? Regardless, help me to have the self-control to stay away from drugs. I know the Bible says my body is the temple of the Holy Spirit. Keep my body pure from anything that will hurt me or dishonor God.

(If you are already using drugs…)

Lord, I need Your help. I didn't plan to, but I started experimenting with drugs. I thought it would be a one-time thing, but now it's become an addiction. Help me to separate myself from this trap. Help my body and mind to heal. I only took drugs to see what it was like. Now I can't stop. I feel so much pressure right now. First, I had pressure in school, now I feel the added pressure from my body longing for more drugs. Free me from my addictions, and place me back on the right path. I know you have a plan for my life. I lay down my cares at your feet and ask you to help. Forgive me for doing this to my body. I want to make my body a holy temple again. Help me to get clean and avoid any further temptation. I ask this in Jesus' Name. Amen.

What does the Bible tell us?

Don't you realize that your body is the temple of the Holy Spirit, who lives in you and was given to you by God? You do not belong to yourself, for God bought you with a high price. So you must honor God with your body. (1 Corinthians 6:19-20)

You say, "I am allowed to do anything"—but not everything is good for you. And even though "I am allowed to do anything," I must not become a slave to anything.(1 Corinthians 6:12)

Everyone must submit to governing authorities. For all authority comes from God, and those in positions of authority have been placed there by God. So anyone who rebels against authority is rebelling against what God has instituted, and they will be punished. (Romans 13:1-2)

And we are instructed to turn from godless living and sinful pleasures. We should live in this evil world with wisdom, righteousness, and devotion to God (Titus 2:12)

"bad company corrupts good character." (1 Corinthians 15:33)

Don't copy the behavior and customs of this world, but let God transform you into a new person by changing the way you think. Then you will learn to know God's will for you, which is good and pleasing and perfect. (Romans 12:2)

Give all your worries and cares to God, for he cares about you. Stay alert! Watch out for your great enemy, the devil. He prowls around like a roaring lion, looking for someone to devour. (1 Peter 5:7-8)

Chapter 8

EATING DISORDERS

E ating disorders can be a difficult topic to discuss. An eating disorder is an unhealthy way of using food to cope with psychological issues. At the risk of stating the obvious, eating disorders are not physically, psychologically, or spiritually healthy. Unfortunately, individuals suffering from an eating disorder are often too embarrassed to seek help. Others are not even aware they have an eating problem. If you have an eating disorder (or know someone who does), please seek medical, psychological, and spiritual help as necessary to treat the problem. Obviously there are many kinds of eating disorders, but let me take a quick moment to provide information that might help you or a friend. Here are the most common types of eating disorders:

Anorexia nervosa: In this disorder, you are intentionally starving yourself. You have a distorted view of your body. Even when you become unusually thin, you still see yourself as overweight. You are so afraid of gaining weight that you simply stop eating. People with this condition may also exercise compulsively. Unfortunately you don't see how dangerously thin you have become, but your friends and family do. Listen to them. They care about you.

Bulimia nervosa: This disorder involves an unhealthy cycle where you overeat (binge) and then "purge" through self-induced vomiting, or laxatives. Anorexia is about stopping food from going "in." Bulimia is about forcing the food "out." Anorexia and Bulimia can both cause many dangerous health issues including loss of muscle tissue, slow heart rate, low blood pressure, unbalanced body fluids, reduced brain function, hair loss, and even loss of your menstrual cycle.

Compulsive Overeating: While Anorexia and Bulimia are defined by not enough food, this condition is about too much food. You eat when you aren't hungry, and spend too much time thinking about food. You struggle with self-control. Compulsive overeaters often "binge," but also "graze." Grazing is when you eat small amounts but frequently return to pick at food throughout the day. Don't fool yourself. Grazing consumes a large amount of calories even if it is only a little at a time. Compulsive overeating leads to weight gain which can lead to serious medical conditions including: diabetes, high blood pressure, high cholesterol, sleep apnea and an increase in chance of heart attack or stroke.

While women are more frequently affected by eating disorders, approximately 10% of men also suffer from eating disorders. Studies suggest as many as 1 out of 4 women will experience an eating disorder at some time in her life.

Now that we know about these eating disorders, let's talk about what causes them. It's a tricky subject because everyone is different. Common contributors include stress, anxiety, and even unhealthy relationships. Other factors include pressure due to sports, dating, and even society's view of "beauty." While many things can trigger these disorders, frequently the root cause is related to feelings of inadequacy and low self-esteem. If you suffer from an eating disorder, you may have a negative view of yourself.

Often an eating disorder is a symptom of something much deeper attacking your mind and heart. To conquer the eating disorder, you need to focus on healing the root cause. If you can heal the root, the rest of the fruit (symptoms, behaviors) can be eliminated. Once you begin to heal the spiritual, the physical can begin to heal as well. Let me share some of the known "roots" of eating disorders.

Control: Often you develop an eating disorder to gain control over your situation. You look in the mirror and don't see the image you want, so you go to desperate measures to get there. Ironically, this desire for control frequently leads to a behavior that is out of control. If you have an eating disorder, you need to give control of your life back to God. Let Him take care of you. He loves you. Trust him and stop trying to do everything yourself. Self-control can be good, but you need to know when to "let go and let God."

Fear: This is one of the key triggers for eating disorders. You are afraid of not being thin enough to be accepted by others. You are afraid of not fitting in with the crowd. Well, the Bible says God did not give you a spirit of fear. That means this fear you are feeling is coming from Satan. Satan wants to incapacitate you with fear. His whole job is to *"steal, kill, and destroy" (John 1:1).* On the other hand, God is love. His love is perfect. The Scriptures say, *"perfect love casts out all fear."* The closer you get to God, the more fear will get pushed out of your life. Maybe it's time to make a change. Why don't you run to God? Surrender your body and heart to Him. He created you. He loves you no matter how you look, but He wants you to be healthy. Tell Him your problems and your dreams, and let Him help. Read the scriptures below aloud and listen to God's promises for you.

Say this prayer...

God, I know my eating habits are out of control. I try, but I can't stop. Please forgive me for trying to control everything. I give my life to You. This includes my body and everything I feed it. I want to be healthy and live a long life. Help me to make right choices. Help me to eat the proper amounts of food. Help me to see myself the way You see me. Place people in my life who can give me assistance. Holy Spirit, I ask for Your divine counsel. Help me find the right path, and pick me up when I fall. I ask this in Jesus' Name. Amen.

What does the Bible tell us?

Don't you realize that your body is the temple of the Holy Spirit, who lives in you and was given to you by God? You do not belong to yourself, for God bought you with a high price. So you must honor God with your body. (1 Corinthians 6:19-20)

And so, dear brothers and sisters, I plead with you to give your bodies to God because of all he has done for you. Let them be a living and holy sacrifice—the kind he will find acceptable. This is truly the way to worship him. Don't copy the behavior and customs of this world, but let God transform you into a new person by changing the way you think. Then you will learn to know God's will for you, which is good and pleasing and perfect. (Romans 12:1-2)

Don't worry about anything; instead, pray about everything. Tell God what you need, and thank him for all he has done. Then you will experience God's peace, which exceeds anything we can understand. His peace will guard your hearts and minds as you live in Christ Jesus. (Philippians 4:6-7)

Give your burdens to the Lord, and he will take care of you. He will not permit the godly to slip and fall. (Psalm 55:22)

Why am I discouraged? Why is my heart so sad? I will put my hope in God! I will praise him again—my Savior and my God! (Psalm 42:11)

He heals the brokenhearted and bandages their wounds. (Psalm 147:3)

So Christ has truly set us free. Now make sure that you stay free... (Galatians 5:1)

Chapter 9

EMPLOYMENT

E very student reaches that moment when you start to think about your future career. You ask yourself, "What kind of job am I going to get?", "Where should I interview?", "How do I know which job to take?", "Where do I want to live?" The whole thing can become overwhelming.

Some of you are fortunate enough to have known since childhood what you wanted to do in life. You want to be an engineer, a teacher, or a doctor. This journey through college is simply to obtain the necessary credentials to fulfill your dreams. Many of you have no idea what the future holds. You may have started with the famous "undeclared" major. You know you need an education, but you're not sure what you want to do for the rest of your life. This is common, so don't worry. Many young people in college are still searching for their place in the world.

The good news is college is often where you first see your future take shape. You may take a certain course and find you really enjoy it. Then you change your major to something using this information or skill. You may meet a new friend or professor who shares an area that resonates with you. You find a stirring inside of you or an excitement at the idea of working in this area. If this epiphany hasn't come yet, it will.

In today's world, the most important step is to finish your college degree. This accomplishment shows any prospective employer you have the dedication and drive to improve yourself and make it through higher education. As a college student, you may view your degree as the end of your race, but it is just the beginning. Your degree will get you a job, but your first job is really a time of learning and gaining real life experience. Afterwards, people ask more about your experience than your degree.

Some of you will step into a career that will keep you fulfilled for years to come. Others will decide your first job didn't feel right, but learn from the experience and find another job that fits you better. Many adults would agree that their current career was not part of their original plan. We find musicians in engineering, and philosophy majors in accounting. The truth is that life is a journey. Your degree is simply a key to open doors. As you progress in your career, you'll find many new doors, and hallways leading to other places. Like a long flowing river, life has twists, turns, and rough waters. There is no simple answer, but knowing God is on your side can ease the burden.

Focus on your studies and trust God. Don't stress about the rest of your life. Just take the next step. Get your degree, talk to your advisors, have some interviews, and let the Lord lead you in the right direction. If you obey Him, and listen to his instruction, He will certainly find you employment. If the first job doesn't interest you, then He'll open another door. The key is to trust Him. Don't try to do all of this on your own. He knows more than you do. Take advantage of His wisdom and allow Him to point you in the right direction. For more encouragement, look at the chapter called "Your Future." For now, look at the Scriptures below for some heavenly advice on finding a job that is right for you.

Say this prayer...

Father, I need Your wisdom and direction in finding a job that is best suited for me. I want to find my place in this world. I want a place where I feel comfortable, appreciated, and successful. Help me not to worry about the past, or the opportunities I may have missed, but to focus on what is Your best for the rest of my life. I want to have a fulfilling job, and be happy. I'm not really sure what to do next. Show me. I need You to open doors of opportunity for me. I lay my future at Your feet and ask You to give me direction, guidance, and favor. I won't worry about anything, but let Your peace be on my heart and mind. You are my source, and I will have confidence, comfort, and encouragement in Your provision. I ask this in Jesus' Name. Amen.

What does the Bible tell us?

Trust in the Lord with all your heart; do not depend on your own understanding. Seek his will in all you do, and he will show you which path to take. (Proverbs 3:6)

For I know the plans I have for you," says the Lord. "They are plans for good and not for disaster, to give you a future and a hope. (Jeremiah 29:11)

The Lord directs the steps of the godly. He delights in every detail of their lives. Though they stumble, they will never fall, for the Lord holds them by the hand. (Psalm 37:23-24)

Commit your actions to the Lord, and your plans will succeed. (Proverbs 16:3)

Commit everything you do to the Lord. Trust him, and he will help you. (Psalm 37:5)

So we can say with confidence, "The Lord is my helper, so I will have no fear. What can mere people do to me?" (Hebrews 13:6)

Seek the Kingdom of God above all else, and live righteously, and he will give you everything you need. (Mathew 6: 33)

Chapter 10

ENCOURAGEMENT

Have you ever felt discouraged? Sure you have. Everyone does from time to time. Let's face it... some days are better than others. It's just a fact. There are days when everything goes great. You do well on an exam and that cute guy or gal talks to you after class. You walk around the rest of the day with a smile on your face. College can be a wonderful time in your life and you will have many fond memories.

Other times you may feel overloaded, unappreciated, and overwhelmed. You miss your high school friends, and your parents, and you feel alone. You wonder if college is worth the hassle. Some of your classes are so difficult. Can you make it? The answer is yes! But don't try it alone. Keep God involved. He is always with you. He's always watching, always listening, and He cares about you. He will always be there to protect you, strengthen you, and support you in whatever is coming your way.

This may sound old fashioned, but the fact is that God has given you the Bible to help you through these times.

You may think the Bible is just full of old stories from long ago. The truth is the Bible is full of life! It is full of hope and encouragement for you. Many of these encouraging Scriptures are included at the end of this chapter. God tells you to be *"strong and courageous,"* and not be *"afraid or discouraged."* He also says He will *"cause everything to work for the good of those who love Him."* He tells us *"anything is possible."* He hears everything you ask Him! You can rely on Him to always keep His word and fulfill any promises He has made.

Faith is your belief in the reality of God's promises. Hope is your expectation that those promises will be fulfilled in your life. Many of us believe in God. The question is whether you believe God will reach out and help you personally. It's easy to have confidence in God but still lose hope. You lose hope because you can't see past your problem. God gives us a simple plan for this: *Trust in the Lord with all your heart; do not depend on your own understanding. Seek his will in all you do, and he will show you which path to take (Proverbs 3:5-6).* In other words, "Don't worry about it." Just talk to Him and He'll show you what to do.

God also makes this one thing clear. If you move closer to Him, He will come closer to you. This just means you should talk to Him more. Let Him know your struggles, and your successes. There's no reason to keep any secrets. He already knows! He just wants you to talk to Him about it. Think of Him as a Father, Protector, Provider, and Friend. He wants to see you happy, successful, and confident. If you let Him into your life and ask for His help, He will surely provide you with answers and encouragement. The Bible tells us "nothing can separate us from God's love." For more encouragement, pray the prayer below and read the verses from God's encouraging Word.

Say this prayer...

Lord, I'm struggling. I seem to have more bad days than good days lately and I'm getting discouraged. I need your help Lord. Help me to know everything is going to be OK. Help me to make the right choices. Help me to make the right decisions to lead me in the direction you want for my life. I'm just feeling a little down. I need to feel Your love and encouragement. Fill me with confidence, happiness, and hope! I ask this in Jesus' Name. Amen.

What does the Bible tell us?

Don't be afraid, for I am with you. Don't be discouraged, for I am your God. I will strengthen you and help you. I will hold you up with my victorious right hand. (Isaiah 41:10)

This is my command—be strong and courageous! Do not be afraid or discouraged. For the Lord your God is with you wherever you go." (Joshua 1:9)

For I can do everything through Christ, who gives me strength. (Philippians 4:13)

"What do you mean, 'If I can'?" Jesus asked. "Anything is possible if a person believes." (Mark 9:23)

And we are confident that he hears us whenever we ask for anything that pleases him. (1 John 5:14)

For I know the plans I have for you," says the Lord. "They are plans for good and not for disaster, to give you a future and a hope. (Jeremiah 29:11)

Keep on asking, and you will receive what you ask for. Keep on seeking, and you will find. Keep on knocking, and the door will be opened to you. (Matthew 7:7)

Chapter 11

FEAR

L ife can be scary. Society can be demanding and the number of choices overwhelming. You may have a fear of failure. You may have a fear of your peers not liking you. Some fear the future. Your fear may focus on personal safety and physical harm. This is especially true today when so much violence is reported in the news. Even simple things like passing your next exam can instill fear. It's only one small event in the big scheme of life, but it can be trau-matizing. Even the pressure of success can be debilitating. What is the root of all this fear? What are we *really* afraid of? Let's examine the basics.

Is all fear bad? Of course not; fear is a real emotion that God instilled in you as a human. It's there to send adrenaline coursing through your veins when you smell fire in your house. It's there to tell you when to flee from danger. Our brains are designed by God to react when danger is present to protect ourselves and loved ones.

However, you can experience another type of fear, and this one isn't healthy. It's what I call "unnatural" fear.

This includes fear of things that haven't happened or don't even exist. You are not worried about "actual" events but "anticipated" events. It's the dread of the first day of school, or the thought of forgetting your words to your solo, or the fear of failing a test. If you are worrying about things that haven't happened, you have an equal chance they won't happen. Don't let the devil steal your peace.

Fear has many faces; it is like an angry beast with many heads. These heads are attached to the same body, the same root, but each of them attacks you differently. The mildest form of fear is called "worry." Worry is a mental distress that results from concern over something you expect to happen. Worry is a subtle type of fear. It causes you to be concerned but not overly so. Worry affects your mind and manifests as nagging negative thoughts you can't seem to shake. Worry is just a word for fear that is more socially acceptable. We even try to disguise worry with words like "concerned" or "apprehensive." People say, "I'm not worried, just concerned." Don't be fooled. Fear is fear, no matter what you call it.

Another form of fear is called "anxiety." Anxiety manifests itself as an overwhelming sense of apprehension. It takes worry to a new level. Anxiety starts in your mind and then moves to the rest of your body. Anxiety is often marked by physiological signs. Your body begins to react to the perceived fear. Your symptoms may include nervousness, increased pulse, upset stomach, butterflies, and more. These individuals live in a constant state of anxiety. Their days may be filled with tension, fatigue, irritability, sleep disturbance, and difficulty concentrating. Like worry, anxiety deals with an imaginary threat and too much energy can be wasted on things that may never happen. Others suffer from acute events of anxiety known as "panic attacks." This is a sudden onset of unexplained apprehension, terror, or impending doom.

We talk of fear as an emotion. What we are really experiencing is a spiritual attack. The Bible says fear is a spirit. The Scripture says, *"For God has not given us a spirit of fear and timidity, but of power, love, and self-discipline."* This verse tells you two things. First, this unnatural fear does not come from God. Secondly, fear is a spirit. A spirit only comes from two sources: God or Satan. In the spiritual world, there is only dark and light. There is no gray. In describing the devil, God tells us *"When he lies, it is consistent with his character; for he is a liar and the father of lies."* This unnatural type of fear originates from lies about the future. I saw an acronym somewhere that said "FEAR" is an acronym for "False Evidence Appearing Real." We know that Satan is behind all this unnatural fear. He tries to strike fear in your heart over something that hasn't happened, and may never happen.

What can we do? First, don't believe the lie. Satan will always say you aren't good enough, smart enough, or pretty enough. He will suggest you will fail, or be hurt, or be embarrassed. God does not want you to live your life in fear. If you are living in fear, then you are not living in faith. God wants you to have faith in Him. He will provide for you, protect you, and guide you into your future. That is, if you let Him. What good is a guide if you leave him behind? What good is a bodyguard if you don't keep him with you? If we truly want to be rid of fear, then we need to embrace God and rebuke the devil.

OK what does this mean exactly? Well it means you should pray and ask God's divine protection and guidance. The Scripture says, *"So humble yourselves before God. Resist the devil, and he will flee from you." (James 4:7)* If God is on your side, you can reject the devil and he can't stay around.

You can fight off this spirit of fear through the Word, and the Name of Jesus.

I wish this was the end of the story, but some form of fear will likely return. God tells us Satan's purpose is to *"steal and kill and destroy." (John 10:10)* He will try to steal your peace, kill your hope, and destroy your dreams. He doesn't give up easily. He will keep trying. Don't let him win. You have the power of the almighty God on your side. He is so much more powerful. Since we are in a war, I recommend that you start every day by putting on the armor of God. The Scriptures below tells you how.

Say this prayer...

Lord, I'm afraid. So many things scare me and I find myself too paralyzed to move forward. Help me to stop worrying. Heal me of my anxiety. Deliver me from all forms of fear. I want You on my side. I want to embrace You as the provider of everything I need. This includes protection from anything the enemy can throw at me. Help me to put on the armor of God to fight the devil and protect me from his sneak attacks. Give me peace Lord. Take away the worry, the strife, the anxiety, the fear of man, and the fear of the future. Help me to stand in confidence knowing You are with me everywhere I go and in everything I do. Thank You for Your protection Lord. From this point forward, I will act in faith and not fear. I ask this in Jesus' Name. Amen.

What does the Bible tell us?

Put on all of God's armor so that you will be able to stand firm against all strategies of the devil. For we are not fighting against flesh-and-blood enemies, but against evil rulers and authorities of the unseen world, against mighty powers in this dark world, and against evil spirits in the heavenly places. Therefore, put on every piece of God's armor so you will be able to resist the enemy in the time of evil. Then after the battle you will still be standing firm. Stand your ground, putting on the belt of truth and the body armor of God's righteousness. For shoes, put on the peace that comes from the Good News so that you will be fully prepared. In addition to all of these, hold up the shield of faith to stop the fiery arrows of the devil. Put on salvation as your helmet, and take the sword of the Spirit, which is the word of God. Pray in the Spirit at all times and on every occasion. Stay alert and be persistent in your prayers for all believers everywhere. (Ephesians 6:11-18)

Even when I walk through the darkest valley, I will not be afraid, for you are close beside me. Your rod and your staff protect and comfort me. (Psalm 23:4)

For God has not given us a spirit of fear and timidity, but of power, love, and self-discipline. (2 Timothy 1:7)

This is my command—be strong and courageous! Do not be afraid or discouraged. For the Lord your God is with you wherever you go." (Joshua 1:9)

So we can say with confidence, "The Lord is my helper, so I will have no fear. What can mere people do to me?" (Hebrews 13:6)

Don't worry about anything; instead, pray about everything. Tell God what you need, and thank him for all he has done. Then you will experience God's peace, which exceeds anything we can understand. His peace will guard your hearts and minds as you live in Christ Jesus. (Philippians 4:6-7)

...be strong and courageous! Do not be afraid and do not panic before them. For the Lord your God will personally go ahead of you. He will neither fail you nor abandon you." (Deuteronomy 31:6)

Chapter 12

FINANCES

F inancial challenges can be especially difficult during your college years. You are paying for your education, your housing, your food, and you don't have a job yet! It's society's rite of passage. If you can make it through all these obstacles, we'll give you a job and the money to pay for what you need. Wouldn't it be great if college were free? You could just focus on your studies and look forward to your future.

Well, I have good news and bad news. First, let me share the bad news. Financial challenges don't go away after college. You may have college loans to pay back. You will also face the delicate task of balancing the amount of money coming in and going out.

Here's the good news. All the hard work you are facing in college is to prepare you for a more lucrative future after college. It's a proven fact that college graduates make higher salaries than those that don't choose college. All this extra time and effort to educate yourself will definitely improve your chances of success. This is the reward.

Here's the best news. You aren't in this alone. God isn't just interested in emotional and spiritual things. He's interested in practical things too. The Bible talks a lot about money and working, and shelter and all the physical things that are important to us. Let me clear up a myth about God and money. Often people misquote the Bible by saying, "money is the root of all evil." When we look at the stock market, politics, sports, and the entertainment industry it might even appear true. However, the real verse actually says, *"the love of money is the root of all kinds of evil."*

Money itself is not evil. Having money is not bad. Being wealthy is not bad. The problem is when you start to love money more than people, or money becomes an idol that replaces God. That's when you get into trouble. People can become obsessed with the constant drive to get more money. Regardless of how much they get, they are never satisfied. Some individuals come into wealth quickly, like those who win the lottery, and lose it just as quickly because they weren't prepared. They didn't have a plan. Many people started from humble beginnings and along the way become incredibly rich. Some of them lose sight of God and start to depend on themselves. When tragedy strikes, they find themselves alone and heart broken. We see examples of this in movie stars, rock stars, etc. They live on the high of being rich and famous, only to fall off the mountain as they become yesterday's news.

Money is necessary to survive almost anywhere in the world. It is simply a means to acquire what you need. We get into trouble when we try to acquire more than we can afford. We start to fall into a trap called "debt." We are bombarded with things on TV we supposedly can't live without. We see the fancy car, bigger house, or designer shoes. Nothing says we can't possess these things, but we need to do it in moderation.

The best thing you can do is develop a financial plan as well as a spiritual plan. Your financial plan should include things like developing a budget, saving for the future, and maybe reaching out to a financial consultant for advice. Understand how much money you will receive from your job, and then subtract the total for all your bills. Whatever is left over must be divided among savings, tithing, investments, and stuff you want to buy.

The spiritual plan is simple. Put your trust in God. In the United States our money even says, "In God we trust"! God says He will "*supply all your needs*," and He will "*never abandon you*." He also says, "*Don't wear yourself out trying to get rich*." Remember, this isn't something you need to do by yourself. God wants to help. He wants you to be successful. I have three children. I want all of them to be successful. What kind of father would want only *some* of his children to prosper? The question you must first ask is this, "Is God really my Father?" If you don't know that answer, go to the chapter on salvation.

Once you've confirmed God is indeed your heavenly Father, it goes without saying you are one of His children. Every good father has financial advice for his children. God's rules are simple. Believe in Him, follow His teachings, put your trust in Him, and give Him your tithe. You may be thinking, "What's a tithe?" It sounds like an old-fashioned term. Well, "tithe" means "a tenth." Another way to say it is "ten percent." God tells us in Malachi 3:10 to bring 10% of your (gross) revenue to Him. Typically, this is given to the local church you attend. God says if you bring this tithe to *His* house, He'll take care of *your* house. If we give Him ten percent, He'll bless the other ninety percent! Seems like a great deal.

Some people get weird about giving money to the church. They get defensive and say the church is only after your money. Don't fall for this lie. If the church were after your money, they would ask for the 90%! The church is simply following the plan God presented long ago. As believers, we are supposed to support the church. The church uses your giving to help widows, orphans, missionaries, and those who need a helping hand. They also use it to bring others to Christ through evangelistic outreach. Our giving helps the church do God's work. This simple plan has worked for thousands of years. Here's the best part. The rest of Malachi 3:10 says that God promises to "*open the windows of heaven*" and "*pour out blessings*" on you for doing this. He even says to "*try it*" so He can prove to you it works. If God is your Father, and you trust Him, then why would you ignore His request? My best financial advice is to trust God and do what He asks. Your life will be full and your finances will be blessed. Let's see what else the Bible says.

Say this prayer...

Lord, I'm worried about my finances. It seems there is never enough to cover my bills. I'm trying to be frugal, but I keep running out of money. Help me to be a good steward of my money. Help me to trust You with my finances. I want my finances to be blessed. I've never tithed before, but I'm willing to try it. I want the windows of heaven to be open over my finances. Most of all I want to follow your advice. I need you to watch over my finances and provide me with favor. Help my money to stretch farther, and provide additional funds to cover my needs. Also, help me find a job after graduation. Open up doors so I can find a great job with a great salary that prepares me for the future. Help me to be in a place where one day I can help others. I ask this in Jesus' Name. Amen.

What does the Bible tell us?

And this same God who takes care of me will supply all your needs from his glorious riches, which have been given to us in Christ Jesus. (Philippians 4:19)

Bring all the tithes into the storehouse so there will be enough food in my Temple. If you do," says the Lord of Heaven's Armies, "I will open the windows of heaven for you. I will pour out a blessing so great you won't have enough room to take it in! Try it! Put me to the test! (Malachi 3:10)

Don't love money; be satisfied with what you have. For God has said, "I will never fail you. I will never abandon you." (Hebrews 13:5)

Wealth from get-rich-quick schemes quickly disappears; wealth from hard work grows over time. (Proverbs 13:11)

Those who love money will never have enough. How meaningless to think that wealth brings true happiness! (Ecclesiastes 5:10)

Don't wear yourself out trying to get rich. Be wise enough to know when to quit. In the blink of an eye wealth disappears, for it will sprout wings and fly away like an eagle. (Proverbs 23:4-5)

"Don't store up treasures here on earth, where moths eat them and rust destroys them, and where thieves break in and steal. Store your treasures in heaven, where moths and rust cannot destroy, and thieves do not break in and steal. Wherever your treasure is, there the desires of your heart will also be. (Matthew 6:19-21)

Chapter 13

FORGIVENESS

Forgiveness is an emotional topic. By its nature, it suggests some sort of personal attack has happened. Someone in your past has done something to hurt you. You may be carrying around a *hurt* in your heart that never healed. This may have happened many years ago, but the pain is still fresh. Perhaps the circumstance didn't hurt as much as it made you *angry*. Now it has festered inside you and created bitterness.

Maybe you have a different situation. You feel *ashamed* about something that happened in your past. You said or did something stupid, and you wish you could take back. Whatever the situation, God wants to fix it. God is literally the King of forgiveness. It's His business. He setup a kingdom based on a few key rules. One of them is forgiveness of sins. God loves you so much that He gave His son Jesus to wipe away the sins of the earth. Because of Jesus, any sin can be forgiven. All you need to do is ask.

Forgiving yourself should really be easy. You are asking God Almighty, the King of the universe, to take away your sins and forget them. He is all-powerful, all-knowing, and omnipresent. You should be confident He can handle it. The problem is that you're embarrassed. You don't want to talk about it with God. You don't want Him to know about your sins. Guess what? He already knows. There are no secrets with God. You just need to trust Him and let Him help. The Bible tells us He not only forgives your sins but forgets them! He will wash away your sins and cleanse you of all unrighteousness.

Then we come to the more difficult part... forgiving someone else. God wants you to forgive others in the same way He has forgiven you. You shouldn't be looking for revenge, or hoping for bad things to happen to those who hurt you. The Bible tells us not to pay back evil with more evil. Judgment of their sins is not your job. Let's leave that to God. Your job is to take on the attitude of Christ, rise above the pain, the anger, and the bitterness, and forgive those that hurt you. This is important for them but also for you. Holding onto anger is like drinking poison and expecting the other person to die. It only hurts you. Forgiving someone can be a wonderfully freeing experience. Let go of the anger and resentment you've carried around for so long. God wants you to forgive them, so He can forgive you. Why wait? Do it today. The scriptures below tell you how.

Say this prayer...

Lord, please forgive me of my sins. I've done some things I'm not proud of and I need a fresh start. Help me to put the past behind, and start living for you. Help me to forgive the people who have hurt me. I want to forgive them, but it still hurts. How do I just let go of what they said and did? I need Your help to forgive them. Take away the pain and the anger and help me really forgive them. I'm ready to leave it all behind and move forward. Give me the strength and compassion to forgive. I ask this in Jesus' Name. Amen.

What does the Bible tell us?

But when you are praying, first forgive anyone you are holding a grudge against, so that your Father in heaven will forgive your sins, too." (Mark 11:24-25)

Never pay back evil with more evil. Do things in such a way that everyone can see you are honorable. (Romans 12:17)

Make allowance for each other's faults, and forgive anyone who offends you. Remember, the Lord forgave you, so you must forgive others. (Colossians 3:12-13)

Then Peter came to him and asked, "Lord, how often should I forgive someone who sins against me? Seven times?" "No, not seven times," Jesus replied, "but seventy times seven! (Matthew 18:21-22)

But if we confess our sins to him, he is faithful and just to forgive us our sins and to cleanse us from all wickedness. (1 John 1:9)

Get rid of all bitterness, rage, anger, harsh words, and slander, as well as all types of evil behavior. Instead, be kind to each other, tenderhearted, forgiving one another, just as God through Christ has forgiven you. (Ephesians 4:31-32)

O Lord, you are so good, so ready to forgive, so full of unfailing love for all who ask for your help. (Psalm 86:5)

Chapter 14

GUILT

Guilt comes in many forms, but it is often due to a poor choice. Maybe you said something careless that upset a friend. Maybe your action caused emotional or physical harm to someone. Your action could be something simple like cheating on your diet, or something more serious like cheating on a test. Perhaps you allowed yourself to become too intimate on a date. Regardless of the circumstance, you feel guilty about what happened. You're ashamed and want to avoid the person connected with that event. You don't want to look into their eyes and find disappointment. You realize what you did was wrong, and you are regretting it.

Guilt comes in different levels of intensity. Guilt can linger in the back of your mind and only show up occasionally. At other times, guilt can be so intense that you find it difficult to concentrate on anything else. You have a knot in your stomach and you can't stop thinking about it.

Have you ever wondered why guilt can be so intense? It is because your flesh is fighting with your spirit. Your flesh wants to do what feels good. It doesn't care if it isn't socially, morally, or legally the right thing to do. We have a sin nature and we sometimes struggle to stay on the narrow path that God has suggested. When we fail, Satan pounces. He loves to see you do something that is against God's will, or hurts someone else. Guilt can be intense because Satan likes to rub it in your face. The Bible calls him the "accuser of the brethren." He loves to remind you of your sins and the punishment you deserve.

Regardless of what caused the guilt, or even what level of guilt you are experiencing, there is one simple solution. The solution is forgiveness. We deserve punishment for our sins, but God has provided a way to avoid punishment. The Bible states that because of Jesus' sacrifice, God will forgive you and cleanse you from unrighteousness. Everyone has sinned, so don't think you are the worst person on earth. We have all done stupid things and made stupid decisions. If needed, ask for forgiveness from the person who you wronged. Then ask God to forgive you and move on.

If you ask for forgiveness, God will forgive your sins, and never think of them again. God is not interested in your baggage. He is interested in your future. He wants you to step back onto the path and move forward. The Bible tells the story of a woman caught in adultery. In those days, this was a crime worthy of the maximum punishment. The church leaders brought her before Jesus. Jesus didn't lecture her for hours and tell her what a bad person she was. She knew what she had done was wrong. He forgave her, then simply said, "*Go and sin no more.*" God is not focused on punishment. He is interested in forgiveness.

The Bible says King David was a man after God's own heart, but he was not a man without sin. He had his share of mistakes and plenty for which to feel guilty. He even became involved in murder and adultery! Later, David took ownership of his actions but didn't let his guilt linger. He knew about God's forgiveness. Read Psalm 51:1-15 and you will see how David prayed to the Lord for forgiveness.

It's time to ask forgiveness for whatever is causing you guilt. Then move forward. Don't drag around that uneasy feeling or hurt. God has forgiven you for your mistake. Move forward in peace and joy knowing that He is the God of second chances. But don't mock God. If you ask for forgiveness, don't turn around and go back to your old ways. That's disrespecting God. Learn from your mistake and move forward with the intent never to repeat it. We're not always successful, but that should be your goal when asking God's forgiveness. Read the scriptures below for more on what God says about this topic.

Say this prayer...

Lord, forgive me for what I did. This guilt is constantly on my mind and I can't let it go. I know what I did was wrong, and I'm sorry. If I've hurt anyone through what I did, please take their hurt away. Please forgive me and cleanse me from my sins. I've learned my lesson and I won't go down that path again. Help me to forgive myself. I knew better but I lacked self-control at the time. Help me to be strong and resist that temptation in the future. Help me get back on the right path and head in the right direction. I want to please You in everything I do. I ask this in Jesus' Name. Amen.

What does the Bible tell us?

Finally, I confessed all my sins to you and stopped trying to hide my guilt. I said to myself, "I will confess my rebellion to the Lord." And you forgave me! All my guilt is gone. (Psalm 32:5)

But if we confess our sins to him, he is faithful and just to forgive us our sins and to cleanse us from all wickedness. (1 John 1:9)

So now there is no condemnation for those who belong to Christ Jesus. (Romans 8:1)

Therefore, since we have been made right in God's sight by faith, we have peace with God because of what Jesus Christ our Lord has done for us. (Romans 5:1)

For everyone has sinned; we all fall short of God's glorious standard. (Romans 3:23)

This means that anyone who belongs to Christ has become a new person. The old life is gone; a new life has begun! (2 Corinthians 5:17)

Brothers, listen! We are here to proclaim that through this man Jesus there is forgiveness for your sins. Everyone who believes in him is declared right with God—something the law of Moses could never do. (Acts 13:38-39)

Chapter 15

HEALING

As humans, we live in a very complicated body. God gave us a wonderfully complex mind, along with a heart that starts beating inside the womb and doesn't stop until your final day on earth. We are amazingly complex, but we live in an imperfect world. Our bodies are affected by the environment, the seasons, our work, our activities, and what we eat. It's not surprising we occasionally get a cold, or the flu, or some kind of infection. Unfortunately, it is sometimes worse than that. Diseases like diabetes and cancer can also affect our bodies.

Here's the good news. God is still in the healing business. God can heal you from any sickness, disease, or condition. The Bible is full of evidence of His healing power. Jesus and the disciples went from town to town healing people. It is still happening today. The world is still full of testimonies as God continues to heal. God is our heavenly Father, and He doesn't want to see His children sick.

Does going to a doctor show a lack of faith? No. God uses doctors, nurses and others in the medical profession.

He has given these individuals wonderful talents for diagnosing the human condition. However, God wants you to reach out to Him first. We know He is always listening to your prayers, and His desire is for you to be healthy.

How do I know God heals us? He talks about it many times in the Bible! Why would the Scriptures say, *"pray for each other so that you may be healed" (James 5:16),* or *"He forgives all my sins and heals all my diseases" (Psalms 103:3)* if it wasn't true?

While God can heal your physical body, He can also heal your mind. He can rescue you from fear, depression, and many other attacks against your mind. You simply ask for His help and trust Him. Several chapters in this book are dedicated to topics related to attacks on your mind such as fear, depression, loneliness, guilt. We all experience these from time to time. If your condition lingers for more than a short time, you need to ask for God's healing. If a mental hurt goes unresolved, it can fester and lead to anger, bitterness, or depression, to name a few. Let God heal your mind as well as your body. If you haven't talked to God recently, maybe it's time for a checkup. Instead of a physical exam, think of it as a "spiritual" exam. Tell Him where it hurts, what isn't working properly, and why you are afraid. He has a great bedside manner and His rates are extremely reasonable. Pray the prayer below and read more about God's healing promises.

Say this prayer...

Lord, I need healing in my body. Something isn't right but I don't know what it is. Reach into my body and fix whatever is causing this pain and discomfort. Heal my body from the top of my head to the bottom of my feet. Remove anything that is impure, and doesn't belong. Restore anything that

has been damaged by infection or disease. Strengthen me
and restore my energy. Take away the fear, and restore my
peace. Father I also ask You to heal my mind. Take away all
the negative thoughts, confusion, fear, and any thoughts that
aren't pleasing to You. I want to be strong in my mind, body,
and spirit. Thank You for healing me. I will praise Your name
for my healing and I will encourage others to reach out to
You. I ask this in Jesus' Name. Amen.

What does the Bible tell us?

*Are any of you sick? You should call for the elders of the church to
come and pray over you, anointing you with oil in the name of the
Lord. Such a prayer offered in faith will heal the sick, and the Lord
will make you well. And if you have committed any sins, you will be
forgiven. (James 5:14-15)*

*Confess your sins to each other and pray for each other so that you
may be healed. The earnest prayer of a righteous person has great
power and produces wonderful results. (James 5:16)*

*He heals the brokenhearted and bandages their wounds.
(Psalm 147:3)*

*Let all that I am praise the Lord; may I never forget the good things
he does for me. He forgives all my sins and heals all my diseases.
He redeems me from death and crowns me with love and tender
mercies. (Psalm 103:2-4)*

*O Lord, if you heal me, I will be truly healed; if you save me, I will be
truly saved. My praises are for you alone! (Jeremiah 17:14)*

He personally carried our sins in his body on the cross so that we can be dead to sin and live for what is right. By his wounds you are healed. (1 Peter 2:24)

O Lord my God, I cried to you for help, and you restored my health. (Psalm 30:2)

Chapter 16

HOMEWORK

Wow. The workload in college is much harder than expected. The professors don't seem to realize you are taking other classes too. How are you going to survive this level of homework? Writing papers, studying for tests and just doing the work required can be so challenging. It can seem overwhelming. You expected college to be difficult, but never really expected it to be this bad.

Is it OK to pray for homework? It seems a bit trivial with all the problems in the world. Why bother God when He's busy with a major crisis somewhere? Well, I have some good news. As a Christian, you serve a God who cares about everything you experience. No task is too little, and no problem too insignificant. God is the Master of multitasking. He can keep the earth spinning, the flowers blooming, and still hear you whisper a prayer.

God's only request is that you do your part. He wants you to work diligently on the problem. He will always reward you if you are trying. Like any father, it makes Him proud to see you doing your best and working towards success. He also wants you to ask for His assistance when you are struggling. We sometimes let our pride get in the way and say, "I don't need anyone's help," but we really do. You may think, "God knows I'm struggling, so why doesn't He do something?" Remember, God doesn't push Himself on anyone. He doesn't force you to accept Him, and He won't force you to ask for His help. The Bible does give plenty of examples where we reach out to Him and He responds. If you ask, He will answer. If you knock, He will open the door. He wants you to reach out in your time of need. The Holy Spirit is your Counselor and Comforter. He wants to help you through your difficult times. You can turn Him when life gets crazy and you feel a bit overwhelmed.

The Bible reminds us when we are tired and weak God is still strong. He will give you the strength you need to make it through the challenge you are facing. Whether it's a difficult teacher, a challenging test, or a lengthy assignment, He will give you the strength and inspiration you need to complete it. He will give you the Wisdom to grasp the things you don't understand.

Let's face it. Sometimes we just need discipline. College is full of distractions, and there is always something more fun than homework. You need to keep the end goal in mind, which is graduating and getting a great job! It's OK to ask God to help you with discipline and remaining focused. He is eager for you to succeed. When you do succeed, give Him praise! Check out more of God's encouraging words below.

Say this prayer...

Lord, this homework is too much for me. I need help! I'm trying, but I'm struggling on some of my classes and I'm afraid my grades may suffer. I need wisdom to understand some of these new concepts. I need a clear mind, void of distractions. I need You to help me to stay focused and have the discipline to make it through this class. Help me with my homework, my tests, and give me the ability to juggle all the things I need to do. I know nothing is impossible with Your help. I ask for Your help in Jesus' Name. Amen.

What does the Bible tell us?

Keep on asking, and you will receive what you ask for. Keep on seeking, and you will find. Keep on knocking, and the door will be opened to you. (Matthew 7:7)

For I can do everything through Christ, who gives me strength. (Philippians 4:13)

For the Lord grants wisdom! From his mouth come knowledge and understanding. (Proverbs 2:6)

Walk with the wise and become wise; associate with fools and get in trouble. (Proverbs 13:20)

Work hard so you can present yourself to God and receive his approval... (2 Timothy 2:15)

If you need wisdom, ask our generous God, and he will give it to you. He will not rebuke you for asking. (James 1:5)

Get all the advice and instruction you can, so you will be wise the rest of your life. (Proverbs 19:20)

Chapter 17

HOPE

Hope is a wonderful thing. It brings joy, happiness, and expectations of a wonderful future. Hope keeps you looking ahead with excitement. Unfortunately, many things can steal your hope. A bad report from the doctor or a bad grade on a test can smother your hope. Maybe it's just the frustration of trying to find Mr. or Ms. Right. Whatever the reason, when you can't see the way out, it is difficult to keep hope alive.

Hope is the desire for something, coupled with the expectation of receiving it. It's not just the "wanting," but also the "expectation" that keeps hope alive. I may still desire to be a professional athlete, but at this stage in life, my expectations are low. Therefore, my hope in that goal is also low. Whereas my desire for a great meal is entwined with the knowledge that my wife is a great cook. My expectation to receive something wonderful for dinner is strong, and my hope is high! Often we keep the desire, but because of circumstances, we lose the hope.

What happens when you lose hope? Maybe your reaction is to feel sad for a few days. Some have a stronger reaction that leads to a serious depression. You may feel like crying, you may feel angry, or you might lose your desire to do anything or go anywhere. For others, losing hope can even lead to suicidal thoughts. Individuals who contemplate suicide often reach a point where they have lost all hope. They don't believe things will improve. Satan loves to kick you when you are down. He will try to convince you the world would be better without you.

How do you fight this hopelessness? You need to renew your attitude of expectation! Where do you find hope when yours has faded? You find hope in the Bible of course! The Scriptures were provided to give you hope and encouragement.

What is the difference between "hope" and "faith"? Faith is related to facts. Faith expects certain events to happen based on promises given to you. We trust our employer to pay us because we made an agreement. When they continue to deliver that paycheck over a long period, our trust grows and we develop faith in the promise they made us. As Christians, our faith is based on the promises God has given us in the Bible. Faith expects things to happen simply because God promised it.

Hope embraces the emotional side of things. Hope focuses on the excitement and anticipation of things to come. It is that feeling of expectation and deep desire for a certain thing to happen. Your hope stands firmly on your faith in God. If your faith is weak, your hope is weak. A strong faith tells you that no matter what lies ahead, God has already been there. God cares about you. You can look forward with hope and excitement about what God will do in your life.

Let's be real for a moment. You can have confidence in God but still lose hope. Why do you lose hope? You lose hope because you can't see a way out of your situation. To grasp hope, you must trust God. To trust God, you must understand His unfailing love for you. God proved His love by allowing His only son to be sacrificed on your behalf. Then He proved His love again, by placing the Holy Spirit inside of you to give you hope. How does the Holy Spirit give you hope? He helps you in your weaknesses. When you don't know how to pray, He intercedes for you.

I know the world is challenging, and like a powerful wind, your hope can be knocked around due to circumstances. You need to tie your hope onto something sturdy so you can remain steadfast. If you place your trust in God, and base your hope on God's word, you will remain steady even in the toughest storm. You will be as an oak tree planted firmly in place with a strong root system.

An important trait to go along with faith, hope, and trust, is patience. God doesn't always do things on your timetable. He sees the bigger picture and His timing is perfect (even when it doesn't seem so to you). Here's how I see it. You are praying for something, and somewhere another person is praying for something related. God may need to address that person's prayer first to make way for your answer. Now consider all the pieces to the puzzle, and you can better understand the logistics God has to handle. We focus on our particular need, while God views the broader solution. Don't lose hope if you don't see immediate results. Fear makes you believe everything has to happen right now. Faith should reassure you that everything will happen in God's perfect timing. Just think of it this way. God is moving stuff around to give you the best result possible.

When you start to lose hope, don't. When you start to feel depressed, look up. Whenever you are discouraged, the Bible says to put your hope in God. Years ago, Don Moen wrote the lyrics to a song called "God will make a way" when he was facing a hopeless situation:

God will make a way,
where there seems to be no way;
He works in ways we cannot see,
He will make a way for me.

He will be my guide,
hold me closely to His side;
With love and strength for each new day,
He will make a way.

It really is that easy. God made you a promise. Now you simply hold on to His promise through faith. God also tells you to grow by learning His Word. As you read the Bible and learn more about God, your hope will increase because He has a message of hope. Remember, God is on your side. The Scriptures tell us nothing can separate you from God's love. Since He loves you, He will take care of you. As you read the Scriptures below, you will see how much God is interested in keeping your hope strong.

Say this prayer...

Lord, restore my hope. Life has been hard lately and I've had some disappointments. I'm tired of worrying about the future. I want to look forward to wonderful things happening in my future. Restore my joy. I want to trust in You only God. Strengthen my faith. Help me to understand You want only the best for me. I know You can see into my future and have a plan for me. Fill me with hope, joy, and peace about my future. I know you have great plans for my life. Help me follow Your path, and restore my hope to overflowing. I ask this in Jesus' Name. Amen.

What does the Bible tell us?

Faith is the confidence that what we hope for will actually happen; it gives us assurance about things we cannot see. (Hebrews 11:1)

I pray that God, the source of hope, will fill you completely with joy and peace because you trust in him. Then you will overflow with confident hope through the power of the Holy Spirit. (Romans 15:13)

You are my refuge and my shield; your word is my source of hope. (Psalm 119:114)

"But blessed are those who trust in the Lord and have made the Lord their hope and confidence. (Jeremiah 17:7)

We can rejoice, too, when we run into problems and trials, for we know that they help us develop endurance. And endurance develops strength of character, and character strengthens our confident hope of salvation. And this hope will not lead to disappointment. For we know how dearly God loves us, because he has given us the Holy Spirit to fill our hearts with his love. (Romans 5:3-5)

Such things were written in the Scriptures long ago to teach us. And the Scriptures give us hope and encouragement as we wait patiently for God's promises to be fulfilled. (Romans 15:4)

For I know the plans I have for you," says the Lord. "They are plans for good and not for disaster, to give you a future and a hope. (Jeremiah 29:11)

Chapter 18

LONELINESS

All your life you've been around your friends. You may have grown up with the same friends from elementary school, through middle school, and into high school. Now, as you graduate and move to college, your friends have gone in different directions. College is exciting, but you feel alone. You've moved to a different town with no friends, no parents, and none of the regular places you used to hang out. It's easy to feel isolated and even abandoned.

The best practical advice I can give is to get involved in a small group. Find a church group, a Bible study, or a student organization where you can connect with others on a regular basis. This will allow you to start to build a network of friends and contacts. Just be sure this group includes individuals who will encourage you, support you, and not lead you in the wrong direction. Your first semester may be a little scary, but life has a way of putting you together with people. You'll meet new friends in class, in church, or even standing in line for coffee. You'll likely have a roommate, and you'll meet their friends. Some of these new friendships will be lifelong relationships. You may even meet your future spouse!

College can seem a bit lonely at the start, but it does get better. The scary part comes from all the unknowns... where the buildings are, where your class is, what your teacher will be like, or if you'll know anyone in your class. These are only beginning butterflies. There's always a bit of angst when you start something new. I promise it will get better.

There is one thing you can count on. You are never alone if God is in your life. It sounds like a cliché, but God is never far away. Even as you read this book, He's watching over you. His job is to protect, provide, and comfort you through all things. Sometimes you need to be loved. He is the Father of Love. Sometimes you want to be comforted. The Holy Spirit is your Comforter and Counselor. Sometimes you want to be safe. God is your refuge, your hiding place, and protects you from trouble.

Whenever you are sad or lonely, take a minute to talk to God. Tell Him what's on your mind. Tell Him the desires of your heart. Maybe you want to meet some friends. Maybe you are looking for someone special with whom to develop a relationship. Perhaps you just want peace in your life. God can help with all of those things.

Some people view God as a divine powerful being who only deals with life or death situations. The truth is God sees everything. He sees the huge storm but also the single tear trailing down your cheek. That's how big God is. He is there for you whenever you are feeling down, or feeling like the last person on earth. There is a song by Luke Garrett that says, *"He loves me... as if I were the only one to love."* That's how God sees us. While He keeps the whole world spinning, He is still interested in what's going on in your life. He wants to hold you in His arms and make things better.

Close your eyes and feel His warm embrace. Let His love flow over you and wash away the fear, hurt, and loneliness. He loves you. It's going to be OK.

Say this prayer...

Lord, I feel very alone. Sometimes the world seems so big and I seem so insignificant. I wonder if I'll make it. I don't have many friends, and I could use some. Help me find some good friends who will support me, and lift me up when I'm down. I just want some friends that I can just have fun with! I need quality friends. Friends who won't lead me the wrong way and will love and respect me. I know You are there for me, and You will watch over me. Give me peace and comfort when I'm feeling lonely. I ask this in Jesus' Name. Amen.

What does the Bible tell us?

Even when I walk through the darkest valley, I will not be afraid, for you are close beside me... (Psalm 23:4)

...For God has said, "I will never fail you. I will never abandon you." So we can say with confidence, "The Lord is my helper, so I will have no fear..." (Hebrews 13:5-6)

"...be sure of this: I am with you always, even to the end of the age." (Matthew 28:20)

And I am convinced that nothing can ever separate us from God's love. Neither death nor life, neither angels nor demons, neither our fears for today nor our worries about tomorrow—not even the powers of hell can separate us from God's love. No power in the sky above or in the earth below—indeed, nothing in all creation will ever be able to separate us from the love of God that is revealed in Christ Jesus our Lord. (Romans 8:38-39)

Don't be afraid, for I am with you. Don't be discouraged, for I am your God. I will strengthen you and help you. I will hold you up with my victorious right hand. (Isaiah 41:10)

My eyes are always on the Lord, for he rescues me from the traps of my enemies. Turn to me and have mercy, for I am alone and in deep distress. (Psalm 25:15-17)

"Look! I stand at the door and knock. If you hear my voice and open the door, I will come in, and we will share a meal together as friends." (Revelation 3:20)

Chapter 19

MARRIAGE

I n college, you are suddenly placed in a new environment with complete strangers. This is a big change from high school. The great thing is that everyone is your age and has a lot in common. You may be from different schools and cities, but you are from the same generation. You've seen the same movies, and you are familiar with the same popular music. It's easy to find things to talk about with your new friends.

One of the bi-products of this unique subset of society is that romantic relationships are often formed during these college years. It's a natural outcome of this rare time in your life. It's the first time as an adult (and likely the last time) that everyone around you is the right age for a potential suitor. Time passes quickly and you meet someone. You have a lot in common and you enjoy spending time together. You start dating and it leads to a serious relationship.

Suddenly you are thinking of marriage. Maybe it's a bit scary. Maybe it wasn't part of your plan. You figured you would get married someday but not this soon. Then there's the added pressure of graduation. It feels as though a deadline has been thrust upon you. You need to make a decision before one of you graduate! Anything can happen after graduation. You could get a job in a different city, or another state! The marriage decision is difficult enough without the additional time pressure.

OK, let's slow down a minute. You should never let anything (or anyone) pressure you into making a decision this important before you are ready. Marriage is a lifelong commitment. Society seems to think it's OK to go in and out of marriage, but God sees marriage as a covenant. This is why wedding vows use words like *"to have and to hold from this day forward, for better for worse, for richer for poorer, in sickness and in health, to love and to cherish, till death us do part."* While these vows aren't specifically in the Bible, they do depict the attitude God wants you to have regarding marriage. God describes marriage as the two of you becoming "one." That's a serious commitment.

God expects men and women to help each another in marriage. We may be equal in God's eyes, but we are designed differently. Aside from the physical aspects, men and women view things differently. Then, each individual has unique strengths and weaknesses. As a married couple, you help support your spouse by filling in the gaps. Like the interweaving of your fingers when you hold hands, you create a unity that is stronger than the sum of its parts. Finding the right person can be a wonderful experience. Marrying the wrong person can be your worst nightmare. Be optimistic, but be wise and proceed with caution.

How do you know if this is the right person for you? I'd wish I could say you will simply know in your heart, but the heart is a tricky thing. It can sometimes get confused between infatuation, love, and lust. The best advice is to pray. Yes, it sounds simple, but it is powerful. Bring God into the discussion. Ask your heavenly Father whether this young man or woman is right for you. Will this person love you, take care of you, and treat you with respect? Ask if they will pray with you over your relationship. You'll find out quickly whether they are serious. If you've already decided on marriage, then pray together about your future. It's a great way to start a lifelong relationship. Examine the Scriptures below to understand what God says about marriage.

Say this prayer...

Lord, I need your help. I wasn't expecting to find someone this soon, but now I think this might be "the one"! I feel loved and respected. I feel so great when I'm around them. I love spending time together and I think we would be good together. I want to take the next step but I'm scared. Help me to know if this is the person I should marry. Help me to know without a doubt that I am making the right decision. I know you can see our future. I know You want the best for both of us. If this person is the right person for me, let me know. If they aren't the right one, let me know that too. Protect my heart. Give me peace and joy in my heart regarding this decision. I ask this in Jesus' Name. Amen.

What does the Bible tell us?

So again I say, each man must love his wife as he loves himself, and the wife must respect her husband. (Ephesians 5:33)

Then the Lord God said, "It is not good for the man to be alone. I will make a helper who is just right for him." (Genesis 2:18)

As the Scriptures say, "A man leaves his father and mother and is joined to his wife, and the two are united into one." (Ephesians 5:31)

Give honor to marriage, and remain faithful to one another in marriage. God will surely judge people who are immoral and those who commit adultery. (Hebrews 13:4)

The man who finds a wife finds a treasure, and he receives favor from the Lord. (Proverbs 18:22)

In the same way, husbands ought to love their wives as they love their own bodies. For a man who loves his wife actually shows love for himself. (Ephesians 5:28)

Don't team up with those who are unbelievers. How can righteousness be a partner with wickedness? How can light live with darkness? (2 Corinthians 6:14)

Chapter 20

OVERWHELMED

Recently a study reported that 94% of college students indicated the best word to describe their life was "overwhelmed." This one topic leads to many of the issues I've covered in this book. Being overwhelmed leads to stress, depression, a lack of hope, and even thoughts of suicide. The world you face today is much more complex than past generations. While your generation has the advantages of the internet, social media, and online shopping, it also faces an increase in the speed of life. The ability to gather information quickly brings with it urgency and pressure. Everyone wants an immediate answer from you. When all those deadlines come together, it is easy to feel overwhelmed.

Being overwhelmed is the result of several elements combined. The first element is related to the _volume_ of tasks or issues. Most of you don't get overwhelmed when you are working on a single task or problem. You may get frustrated but not overwhelmed. We get overwhelmed when we have to juggle *multiple* problems.

The second issue is related to the element of *time*. You aren't overwhelmed when you have plenty of time to complete something. The real concerns start when you have a limited amount of time to complete the task. The world keeps adding pressure to speed up things. Everything from fast food to purchasing stock has the pressure to move faster.

The third element has to do with your *skills*. This speaks to your capacity to understand the problem and develop a solution. Let's be real. We have different abilities. Some of you are good at math. Others are good with your hands. For some, music comes easily while others are gifted in sports. We are all made wonderfully different by our Creator, but we are all given unique gifts. Unfortunately, the big plot twist in life is that your problems don't always match your gifting. While these challenges may cause the stretching and growing you need in life, they can also contribute to feeling overwhelmed. You are out of your comfort zone, but still face the looming deadline to complete the task.

This brings me to the final piece of the puzzle. You need the right tools and resources to solve your problem. If math isn't your thing, get a calculator, or a tutor. If you can't tell directions, buy a compass or use your smart phone. If you don't know how to fix your hot water heater, call a plumber. For this generation, you always have YouTube!

Many elements contribute to feeling overwhelmed. Perhaps you have too much to do, and not enough time to do it. Maybe you don't have enough knowledge for the task, and nobody to help to solve the problem. Any of those combinations can leave you exhausted. Here's another truth. Certain individuals are better at multitasking than others. Some are able to juggle multiple things every day and segment your brains to process the tasks in parallel. That's how we get generals and CEOs. Many of you are wired to focus on one thing at a time and do a quality job. By now, you probably know which type you are. Don't worry if you struggle in this area. Everybody needs help in something. Even the greatest leaders who handle multiple problems and millions of dollars still struggle with something. We all get overwhelmed; the things that overwhelm us are just different.

Here's the good news. You don't have to handle all of this alone. You have access to a supernatural helper. The Bible says Jesus will help carry your burdens and give you rest. When you don't know what to do, the Bible says cry out to the Lord for help. He is the source of your strength. He will provide wisdom, guidance, rest, and protection. He never gets tired. If you are feeling overwhelmed, pray this prayer and then meditate on the scriptures following.

Say this prayer...

Lord, I'm crying out for your help. I'm overwhelmed. I have so much to do and I don't know where to start. I need direction. I need your wisdom. I can't handle all of this myself. I ask You to remove this burden from my shoulders and carry it for me. I want to do my part, but I can't handle the pressure. I need relief. Please give me strength, peace, and rest. I know that I can handle this with Your help, but I can't do it alone. Thank You so much for being there for me. Thank You for caring enough about me and my problems that You offer to carry the load on my behalf. Even as I pray this prayer and take a deep breath, I feel peace flooding over me just knowing that You are there. Thank You for loving me. I ask this in Jesus' Name. Amen.

What does the Bible tell us?

The Lord helps the fallen and lifts those bent beneath their loads. (Psalm 145:14)

Give all your worries and cares to God, for he cares about you. (1 Peter 5:7)

Then Jesus said, "Come to me, all of you who are weary and carry heavy burdens, and I will give you rest. Take my yoke upon you. Let me teach you, because I am humble and gentle at heart, and you will find rest for your souls. (Matthew 11:28-29)

When I am overwhelmed, you alone know the way I should turn... (Psalm 142:3)

Commit everything you do to the Lord. Trust him, and he will help you. (Psalm 37:5)

This is my command—be strong and courageous! Do not be afraid or discouraged. For the Lord your God is with you wherever you go." (Joshua 1:9)

The Lord directs the steps of the godly. He delights in every detail of their lives. Though they stumble, they will never fall, for the Lord holds them by the hand. (Psalm 37:23-24)

Chapter 21

PARENTS

People seem to have mixed feelings about their parents. Some kids live for their parents, and others can't wait to move away. I don't know what your relationship has been with your parents, but they are rooting for you. They will miss you as you go off to college, but they are excited to see you reach your potential. Every parent has hopes and dreams for their children, and longs for them to be happy and content.

Sometimes you disagree with your parents, but remember they only want the best for you. Parents have the responsibility to provide shelter, finances, clothing, education, and anything else you need to be healthy and successful. This includes advice, counseling, and guidance on how to stay on the right path. It's not that they don't want you to be independent. They bear the responsibility to keep you on the narrow path and out of trouble. Things get tense when they see you stepping outside the boundaries. They want to offer guidance until you can handle life on your own. Remember, maturity is not defined by a number.

Reaching the age of 18 or 21 does not make you mature. Maturity takes time, experience, and advice. Parents are simply trying their best to prepare you.

No parents are perfect. They struggle, make bad decisions, and lose their tempers, but the reason for their intervention in your life is a mixture of love and responsibility. Your parents love you very much, even though they may not be great at communicating it. They feel responsible for preparing you to take on the world. Some parents let go too early, and others don't know when to let go, but they are trying. Really they are. Give them a break. Don't argue over everything and don't rebel to prove a point. Show them love, respect, and appreciation. You may not always understand it, but they deserve it.

I'm sure you've heard of the "Ten Commandments." These were rules God gave the Israelites many years ago. They were the "top ten" rules, and they included things like *"Thou shalt not kill"* and *"Thou shalt not commit adultery."* These were serious rules God setup to keep everyone on the right path. Right there alongside murder, you'll find this one: *"Honor your father and mother."* God gave His followers a list of things most important to Him, and He included treating parents with respect. Nobody argues with the other rules, so why do we often ignore this rule about parents? This commandment even comes with a promise! God said if you honor your parents, you would *"live a long and full life." (Exodus 20:12)*

Maybe your relationship with your parents is wonderful, or maybe your relationship is a bit rocky. The Bible encourages you to fix it. Pick up the phone. Don't text them. Call your parents and tell them you love them and appreciate everything they've done for you. Then ask Mom to make your favorite dessert. That will make her smile. The scriptures below will help you understand how important your relationship to your parents is.

Say this prayer...

Lord, forgive me for not honoring my parents. I know they love me. I just get frustrated with them sometimes. I want to make my own decisions and sometimes they still treat me like a child. I know they mean well. Help me to honor them for who they are, and appreciate them for what they've done for me. I forgive them for those times when we didn't agree, and I ask for forgiveness for the times I didn't listen. Help us build a healthy relationship. I know they only want what is best for me. As I honor and respect them, help them to understand and support my dreams. I ask this in Jesus' Name. Amen.

What does the Bible tell us?

"Honor your father and mother. Then you will live a long, full life in the land the Lord your God is giving you. (Exodus 20:12)

Children, always obey your parents, for this pleases the Lord. (Colossians 3:20)

My child, listen when your father corrects you. Don't neglect your mother's instruction. (Proverbs 1:8)

Children, obey your parents because you belong to the Lord, for this is the right thing to do. "Honor your father and mother." This is the first commandment with a promise: If you honor your father and mother, "things will go well for you, and you will have a long life on the earth." (Ephesians 6:2-3)

A wise child accepts a parent's discipline; a mocker refuses to listen to correction. (Proverbs 13:1)

The father of godly children has cause for joy. What a pleasure to have children who are wise. So give your father and mother joy! May she who gave you birth be happy. (Proverbs 23:24-25)

Honor your father and mother, as the Lord your God commanded you. Then you will live a long, full life in the land the Lord your God is giving you. (Deuteronomy 5:16)

Chapter 22

PATIENCE

There is an old joke that says, "I want patience, and I want it right now!" Sometimes we all feel that way. We struggle with long lines, slow people, and frustrating situations. We are in a hurry and we need life to move faster.

Society is moving at a faster and faster pace. We went from home cooked meals to fast food. Then fast food got drive through service, but even that wasn't fast enough. We rush through life in fear of missing something. The musical group Alabama has a lyric in one of their songs that goes like this:

I'm in a hurry to get things done
Oh I rush and rush until life's no fun
All I really gotta do is live and die
But I'm in a hurry and don't know why

That's the way it is sometimes. Life keeps pushing you to accomplish more in a smaller amount of time. You rush around school and when you return home, it's difficult to relax. Your mind is still focused on the hustle and bustle of the day. Christians aren't exempt. You will endure your share of frustrations. When something or someone gets in your way, you may get frustrated. You may even lash out with harsh words or gestures. You may lose your patience with strangers, co-workers, and even those closest to you.

The Scripture says that those difficult times develop your character and strengthen you. God wants you to rise above the frustration. The Bible tells you to be *"quick to listen, slow to speak, and slow to get angry." (James 1:19)* It also tells you to respect other people and be kind and patient even with difficult people.

Seriously? God wants you to be patient even with the difficult people? Doesn't He understand you get frustrated too? Sure He does. The catch is that you have a responsibility others don't. The Bible says people will know you are a Christian by your love. This includes how you treat people. This means everyone. If you get angry and lash out like everyone else, then what example are you setting? If you keep your cool even in frustrating situations, people will ask, "How do you do it?", "How do you stay calm?" Then you tell them about your relationship with God. God wants you to be tenderhearted, kind, gentle, and patient. He wants you to love others because He is the Father of love. He wants you to represent Him well, so others will be drawn to Him too.

In your relationship with God, the Bible encourages you to be still and wait for Him. If trouble comes, you should keep praying and be confident He will come to your rescue. Sometimes you may get frustrated with "doing the right thing" but not seeing any difference. God tells you not to get tired of doing good. If you don't give up, you'll see the blessings. If you have patient endurance, and continue to do His will, then you will receive what He has promised you. Check out the Scriptures below to see God's comments about patience.

Say this prayer...

Lord help me to be patient. Help me to show compassion, mercy, love, and forgiveness to others. Help me with my anger. I'm just so frustrated sometimes. I know I should have better control of my emotions. Help me with my self-control. Give me peace in the midst of frustrating circumstances, and help me to remember that my trust is in You. I know You are watching over the big picture, and all these tedious tasks I have aren't worth getting upset about. Give me a new perspective on life. Give me a new hope, and gentleness towards others. I ask this in Jesus' Name. Amen.

What does the Bible tell us?

Always be humble and gentle. Be patient with each other, making allowance for each other's faults because of your love. (Ephesians 4:2)

Since God chose you to be the holy people he loves, you must clothe yourselves with tenderhearted mercy, kindness, humility, gentleness, and patience. Make allowance for each other's faults, and forgive anyone who offends you. Remember, the Lord forgave you, so you must forgive others. (Colossians 3:12-13)

Rejoice in our confident hope. Be patient in trouble, and keep on praying. (Romans 12:12)

So let's not get tired of doing what is good. At just the right time we will reap a harvest of blessing if we don't give up. (Galatians 6:9)

We also pray that you will be strengthened with all his glorious power so you will have all the endurance and patience you need. (Colossians 1:11)

May the Lord lead your hearts into a full understanding and expression of the love of God and the patient endurance that comes from Christ. (2 Thessalonians 3:5)

Patient endurance is what you need now, so that you will continue to do God's will. Then you will receive all that he has promised. (Hebrews 10:36)

Chapter 23

PEACE

It seems like the news is always full of war, and rumors of war. Then, the reports of school shootings are almost too much to bear. If you allow it, the violence and stress of this world can take away your peace. Don't let that happen. As Christians, we know God is in control. We know He is watching over us, and we must continue to tell others about the protection and peace that can be found with Him.

Sometimes peace isn't related to civil unrest and political conflict. Sometimes your lack of peace is in your own heart, or in the pit of your stomach. For reasons known to you, or sometimes unknown, you don't feel at rest. Inside you are anxious and unsettled.

So, how do you find true peace? Many people search for peace in all the wrong places. They look for answers in drugs, Eastern meditation, and even psychics. The only real answer to peace is Jesus. He is the Prince of Peace. When Jesus came into the world, he brought peace between man and God through his sacrifice on the cross. He positions himself between you and your enemies to protect you from danger.

You must give your concerns to God and let Him fight your battles. The Bible says He will supply peace to those who trust Him. If you continue to worry and carry around your burdens, are you really showing trust? The Scripture says He will give you peace of mind and heart. This is a supernatural peace you can't get anywhere else. This peace is only available from God. He is so confident in this He says, *"Don't be troubled or afraid."* There is one catch. God supplies this peace for those who are committed to Him. This gift is for those who love and trust Him.

Here is a simple illustration. Let's say are a famous person and have a personal bodyguard. The bodyguard's job is to watch over you. His job is to protect you and keep trouble from getting near you. This allows you to enjoy life without worrying about what may sneak up behind you. This protector isn't responsible for everyone, just you. You have a contract for his services. In the same way, when you accept Jesus, you sign a spiritual contract with God. You join His family and He becomes your Father and protector. As part of the family, you receive all the gifts and benefits He has for His children. You can't expect God's peace if you don't believe and trust in Him. He will take care of you and give you peace, if you let Him.

God's message is simple. If you do your part, He'll do His part. If you pray, He will listen. If you accept Jesus, He will provide salvation. The Father's door is always open, but it starts with His son Jesus. If you ask for help, He'll deliver. If you ask for peace, He will supply a peace so amazing you can't even comprehend how it's possible. The Bible describes it this way, *"Then you will experience God's peace, which exceeds anything we can understand."*

(Philippians 4:7). Read below to find more of God's promises about peace.

Say this prayer...

Lord, I'm anxious. I always feel a bit nervous about what is going to happen. I don't want to live in fear. Please fill my life with peace. Restore joy and happiness to my life. I want to live a life of confidence. I want people to see peace, joy, and love within me. I want them to ask how I can be so happy. I want the confidence to tell them about you. Restore my peace Lord. I trust You and I ask for Your peace that surpasses all understanding. I ask this in Jesus' Name. Amen.

What does the Bible tell us?

"Submit to God, and you will have peace; then things will go well for you. Listen to his instructions, and store them in your heart. (Job 22:21-22)

You will keep in perfect peace all who trust in you, all whose thoughts are fixed on you! (Isaiah 26:3)

"I am leaving you with a gift—peace of mind and heart. And the peace I give is a gift the world cannot give. So don't be troubled or afraid. (John 14:27)

I pray that God, the source of hope, will fill you completely with joy and peace because you trust in him. Then you will overflow with confident hope through the power of the Holy Spirit. (Romans 15:13)

Now may the Lord of peace himself give you his peace at all times and in every situation. The Lord be with you all. (2 Thessalonians 3:16)

Don't worry about anything; instead, pray about everything. Tell God what you need, and thank him for all he has done. Then you will experience God's peace, which exceeds anything we can understand. His peace will guard your hearts and minds as you live in Christ Jesus. (Philippians 4:6-7)

For God is not a God of disorder but of peace... (1 Corinthians 14:33)

Chapter 24

PERSEVERANCE

S ometimes you feel like giving up. The battle has been too tough, or your path forward seems filled with too many obstacles. We've all been there. You stand at the crossroads (or sometimes a dead end). You have a choice to move forward and climb that wall, or to take the easier path. It's easy to stop and turn around. Perseverance is about forging ahead until you succeed.

Having difficult times isn't unusual. The Bible tells us troubles will come, but you should learn from them. Problems help your faith to grow. I heard someone say once, "*The struggle you're in today is developing the strength you need for tomorrow.*" That's why the Scripture says to consider it an opportunity when troubles come your way. When you deal with problems, you must exercise your faith. When you exercise your faith, it gets stronger. In fact, every time you persevere you gain confidence you can succeed next time.

What does the Bible tell us? God encourages you to push past the obstacles. He says things like "*anything is possible." He tells you to be "*strong and courageous*." He asks you to "*hold on tightly without wavering*," and lets you know He can be trusted to keep His promises. He encourages you to be confident, patient, and keep on praying. The Bible also confirms that God will never leave you nor forsake you.

When you find yourself in one of those difficult situations that seem insurmountable, just realize you have a divine partner at your side. As you stare at the obstacle ahead of you, He can give you a supernatural boost to get you over the top. However, like most things with God, He wants you to ask. In the famous "Sermon on the Mount," Jesus talked about the virtue of perseverance. He said if you asked, He would answer. If we knocked, then He would open the door. The context of this Scripture refers to a "continuous action." Jesus is telling you to keep on asking, keep on seeking, and keep on knocking. This persistence in seeking God's help is what will pull you across the finish line.

The Bible states that with Christ you can do everything because he will give you strength. As you look to your future, you can have confidence you will succeed. As you look into the past, you'll see He has been with you all the way. *"Jesus Christ is the same yesterday, today, and forever." (Hebrews 13:8)* Check out the other encouraging scriptures below.

Say this prayer...

Lord I need your help. I'm facing some very difficult problems. Help me make the right decisions. Give me direction on which path I should take. Provide me with a solution to conquer the challenges in front of me. I know nothing is too small for Your attention, and nothing is too large for You to handle. Help me face this challenge and be successful. Help me not to get in the way of Your wisdom. If You want me to go around it, let me know. If You want me to confront it head on, let me know. If You want me to take an alternate path, let me know. I know I can make it through this difficult time with Your help. I ask this in Jesus' Name. Amen.

What does the Bible tell us?

Keep on asking, and you will receive what you ask for. Keep on seeking, and you will find. Keep on knocking, and the door will be opened to you. For everyone who asks, receives. Everyone who seeks, finds. And to everyone who knocks, the door will be opened. (Matthew 7:7-8)

Dear brothers and sisters, when troubles of any kind come your way, consider it an opportunity for great joy. For you know that when your faith is tested, your endurance has a chance to grow. So let it grow, for when your endurance is fully developed, you will be perfect and complete, needing nothing. If you need wisdom, ask our generous God, and he will give it to you. He will not rebuke you for asking. (James 1:2-5)

Trust in the Lord with all your heart; do not depend on your own understanding. Seek his will in all you do, and he will show you which path to take. (Proverbs 3:5-6)

We also pray that you will be strengthened with all his glorious power so you will have all the endurance and patience you need. May you be filled with joy, always thanking the Father. He has enabled you to share in the inheritance that belongs to his people, who live in the light. (Colossians 1:11-12)

As for the rest of you, dear brothers and sisters, never get tired of doing good. (2 Thessalonians 3:13)

God blesses those who patiently endure testing and temptation. Afterward they will receive the crown of life that God has promised to those who love him. (James 1:12)

For I can do everything through Christ, who gives me strength. (Philippians 4:13)

Chapter 25

PORNOGRAPHY

In the days before the internet, the only access to pornography was through "adult" magazines. These magazines were placed high on a shelf away from children. The covers were obscured with brown paper to hide the images. If you decided to buy one of these magazines, you had to endure the embarrassment of facing the checkout clerk.

Today, many of these barriers are gone. The internet provides easy, anonymous access to pornography. Society has also become more accepting of nudity and sexually explicit material. This is evident in movies and even prime time television. The moral guidelines continue to be diluted until almost anything is accepted.

The temptations of young people today, are not that different from previous generations. Sin and lust have been around for a very long time. The difference is the increase in acceptance and availability of pornography. Past generations didn't have easy access to pornography. Today it's available at the click of a mouse. You must make a moral choice to avoid these lustful images.

Let's be honest. The majority of pornography is consumed by men. Men are more "visual" in nature. Pornographers and even advertisers understand this. They use pictures that pique your interest to get you to buy their products. Being naughty or risqué has even become fashionable for young women. The provocative clothing of prominent entertainers has contributed to this trend. Women feel pressured to reveal more skin to attract men. Nobody wants to be seen as a "prude." Society wants to break down the barriers and remove all censorship rules. Regardless of popular opinion, this idea does not line up with God's plan. God created rules to protect us. He gave us guidelines to keep ourselves pure and avoid temptation.

While pornography was once limited to magazines and movies, it has slithered into people's personal lives. New fads like "sexting" (where men and women send nude pictures of themselves to their boyfriends/girlfriends) have invaded our society. This may sound old-fashioned, but there is no reason for anyone but your spouse to see you naked. Technically, this falls into the category of pornography. People say, "Those photos were private!" You may think it was private, but those pictures have a way of getting around to others long after you break up with that person. Don't do it.

Just because this pornography didn't lead to actual sex doesn't mean you are innocent. The Bible says that even thinking sexually about a person who is not your spouse is a sin. I dare say looking at pornography leads to that type of thinking. This isn't just about being conservative. God's rules were made to protect you. God wants to keep you safe and healthy. He wants your body and mind to be pure. He also wants you to build Godly relationships. Check out the Scriptures below to understand more.

Say this prayer...

God, help me to control my desire to view pornography whether it is books, magazines, television, movies, or the internet. Lead me away from the temptation when those times come. Help me to have self-control and keep my thoughts on Godly things. I want to live a life that honors you. Help me to rise above the pressures of society, and the temptations of my own flesh. I ask this in Jesus' Name. Amen.

What does the Bible tell us?

Temptation comes from our own desires, which entice us and drag us away. These desires give birth to sinful actions. And when sin is allowed to grow, it gives birth to death. (James 1:14-15)

For the world offers only a craving for physical pleasure, a craving for everything we see, and pride in our achievements and possessions. These are not from the Father, but are from this world. (1 John 2:16)

But I say, anyone who even looks at a woman with lust has already committed adultery with her in his heart. (Matthew 5:28)

How can a young person stay pure? By obeying your word. (Psalm 119:9-10)

When you follow the desires of your sinful nature, the results are very clear: sexual immorality, impurity, lustful pleasures... (Galatians 5:19)

Because we belong to the day, we must live decent lives for all to see. Don't participate in the darkness of wild parties and drunkenness, or in sexual promiscuity and immoral living... (Romans 13:13)

God's will is for you to be holy, so stay away from all sexual sin. Then each of you will control his own body and live in holiness and honor— not in lustful passion like the pagans who do not know God and his ways. (1 Thessalonians 4:3-5)

Chapter 26

PREGNANCY

While pregnancy is a cause for celebration in married couples, for a young unmarried person it can be a scary situation. Unfortunately, this is happening to an increasing number of young people. I want to be real with you, so I'm going to give you some stern advice, but stay with me because there is good news.

We really need to address two separate issues. The first issue is premarital sex. Let's make it simple. If you don't have sex, you don't need to worry about anyone becoming pregnant. Abstinence is still the only sure form of birth control. It's as simple as that. I'll share more on the subject of sex in a later chapter.

The second issue is what to do now that you are pregnant. While politicians and the media provide many opinions, there is only one truth. God says all human life is sacred. Most of you know the Ten Commandments include "Thou shalt not kill."

God created a miraculous process that takes the tiniest substance from men and women and creates life. This amazing process creates a new life at conception. Since Adam and Eve, every human has been produced through this process. Pregnancy isn't about God letting something bad "happen" to you. He simply allowed the creation of new life to take place. If you participated in unprotected sex, you made a choice to gamble on the outcome. Now you are dealing with the consequences of the choice you made. Young people never intend to get pregnant, but whenever they have sex, they take on the risk of several consequences including sexually transmitted diseases and unwanted pregnancy.

Pregnancy was never meant to be a negative thing. It is not a disease, or a condition you should want to get rid of like the flu. God put this whole process in order. This is His plan. This is why sex is intended for married couples. Marriage is a commitment between a man and woman who want to spend the rest of their lives together. Sex was designed for that kind of loving environment because He wanted babies to have a nurturing environment in which to prosper. Sex wasn't meant for two people who are complacent to spend one lustful night together.

In the beginning, God created basic rules like "gravity." Gravity works whether you want it to or not. If you jump off a cliff, you can't blame God for falling. When you take part in an act designed for producing children, you shouldn't blame Him for your pregnancy. You don't have the right to end that life for your *convenience*. Your unborn child should not be the victim of your poor decision.

In many Scriptures, God talks about the sanctity of life. If you are pregnant right now and considering an abortion, I ask you to reconsider. It isn't the child's fault. Your baby deserves a life of its own. Consider carrying your child to term, and raising the child in a loving home. Do whatever is needed. Get help from your parents, grandparents, family, church, or friends. If you aren't able to raise the child, then please consider adoption. There are caring people out there who will nurture them and give them the love they deserve.

Some of you have already been through an abortion. No matter what your circumstance was, ending your pregnancy can be a traumatic event. You may carry guilt, shame, depression, or sadness for years afterwards. If no one has told you, let me be the first. God still loves you. He can take away your sadness. He can heal that pain deep inside you. He is the giver of life, but He is also the Father of forgiveness. He will forgive you. Ask Him right now.

Regardless of whether you abandoned a pregnancy in the past, or you are unmarried and pregnant right now. God will forgive you. Just ask Him. Remember, you are His child. He loves you and cares about what happens to you. Here's the amazing thing about God. He has no grandchildren, only more children. Please bring the child you are carrying into the world because that's His child too. He can help. Choose one of the prayers below and then look at the wonderful scriptures related to this topic.

Say this prayer...

(If you are unmarried and pregnant)
God, I never thought it would happen to me, but I'm pregnant. I'm scared and embarrassed, and I don't know what to do, so I'm asking for Your help. I can't do this on my own. Please forgive me of my sin, and help me to deliver this baby. Give me direction, wisdom, and provide help from my friends and family. I know You love me, and You love my baby. Thank You for watching over us and protecting us. I ask this in Jesus' Name. Amen.

(If you are unmarried and the father)

Lord, forgive me for my sin. I never intended to get anyone pregnant. I'm not sure what to do now. I take equal responsibility for this unborn child. Please give me wisdom and direction on how to fulfill my duty as the father. Help me work through this with the child's mother. Help us to do what is best for the baby. Help me to learn from this and walk in your ways. I ask this in Jesus' Name. Amen.

(If you have had an abortion)

Lord, I'm so sorry for what I've done. I was scared, and I didn't know what else to do. Now I understand it was wrong. I didn't think about the life I was ending, I was just focused on my own needs. I ask for your forgiveness. I know you don't hold this against me. Help me to forgive myself. Help me to overcome the guilt and the sadness. Forgive me and make me whole again. I ask this in Jesus' Name. Amen.

What does the Bible tell us?

"I knew you before I formed you in your mother's womb... (Jeremiah 1:4-5)

You made all the delicate, inner parts of my body and knit me together in my mother's womb. Thank you for making me so wonderfully complex! Your workmanship is marvelous—how well I know it. You watched me as I was being formed in utter seclusion, as I was woven together in the dark of the womb. You saw me before I was born. Every day of my life was recorded in your book. Every moment was laid out before a single day had passed. (Psalm 139:13-16)

Children are a gift from the Lord; they are a reward from him. (Psalm 127:3)

For I can do everything through Christ, who gives me strength. (Philippians 4:13)

It will be like a woman suffering the pains of labor. When her child is born, her anguish gives way to joy because she has brought a new baby into the world. (John 16:21)

Don't be afraid, for I am with you. Don't be discouraged, for I am your God. I will strengthen you and help you. I will hold you up with my victorious right hand. (Isaiah 41:10)

Yet you brought me safely from my mother's womb and led me to trust you at my mother's breast. I was thrust into your arms at my birth. You have been my God from the moment I was born. (Psalms 22:9-10)

Chapter 27

PROTECTION

Life can be intense. You hear about things on the news like robberies, shootings, and home invasions. The world can seem scary at times. Most of your life you've lived with your parents and had someone there to protect you. Now, you are on your own and suddenly feel vulnerable. The good news is that you have a protector. He commands an army of angels to watch over His children.

Because of where I live, I've been through several hurricanes. These violent storms can topple trees, flood the streets, and literally blow down your house. While I always took the normal precautions of boarding up windows and bringing in the lawn furniture, I never suffered the debilitating fear that some experience during the storm. I always knew God was watching over my home and family. I knew because I asked for His help. You are entitled to certain blessings by being one of God's kids. The Bible says He will be your shelter. He is your refuge in times of trouble and will provide you with a place of safety in His arms.

Maybe what scares you the most is someone trying to hurt you. Violence is on the news every night. When I was a child, hearing a siren drew you to the front porch to see what was happening. Now, people barely lift an eyebrow. Society is becoming accustomed to hearing about violence and we are becoming desensitized about the impact to others. Maybe certain thoughts come to you when you are alone. *"What if someone broke into my apartment?" "What if someone tried to grab me when I'm walking home from school?"* This fear of what "might" happen can be debilitating.

Here is my advice. Don't worry because worry won't help. Do pray because prayer will help. Prayer is simply talking to God. If you tell God your fears, and ask him to protect you, then you have commissioned an army of angels to watch over you. One angel can handle anything you would encounter here on Earth. God has thousands at His command.

I have two daughters. The eldest is living in another city. For the first time in my life, I'm not there to protect her. This is uncomfortable for me. It is easy to let worry creep into my thoughts. Then I remember. I can call on God to protect her even if she is away from me. He has much more powerful resources at His disposal. I've also taught her to pray. Now both of us are praying for her protection.

The Bible says He is a rock, a shield, a fortress, a place of safety. He never sleeps. That's the kind of security God offers. Tell Him when you are afraid. Ask Him for protection and then sleep soundly knowing He is always watching over you. The scriptures below tell you how great a protector He really is.

Say this prayer...

Lord, I'm scared. Sometimes I'm scared and I don't even know why. I pray for your protection. I know I can ask your angels to watch over me. Because it is your will for me to be safe, I know you hear my prayers. Protect me from anything or anyone who would try to cause me harm. I pray against the devil trying to torment me with fear. The Bible says fear is not from God, so I will not linger on any scary thoughts. Fill my mind with peace and confidence. Protect me from anything or anyone that would try to harm me. I ask this in Jesus' Name. Amen.

What does the Bible tell us?

...Be strong in the Lord and in his mighty power. Put on all of God's armor so that you will be able to stand firm against all strategies of the devil. For we are not fighting against flesh-and-blood enemies, but against evil rulers and authorities of the unseen world, against mighty powers in this dark world, and against evil spirits in the heavenly places. Therefore, put on every piece of God's armor so you will be able to resist the enemy in the time of evil. Then after the battle you will still be standing firm. (Ephesians 6:10-13)

The Lord is my rock, my fortress, and my savior; my God is my rock, in whom I find protection. He is my shield, the power that saves me, and my place of safety. (Psalm 18:2)

For you are my hiding place; you protect me from trouble... (Psalm 32:7)

The Lord says, "I will rescue those who love me. I will protect those who trust in my name. (Psalm 91:14)

My God is my rock, in whom I find protection. He is my shield, the power that saves me, and my place of safety. He is my refuge, my savior, the one who saves me from violence. I called on the Lord, who is worthy of praise, and he saved me from my enemies. (2 Samuel 22:3-4)

Even when I walk through the darkest valley, I will not be afraid, for you are close beside me. Your rod and your staff protect and comfort me. (Psalm 23:4)

But the Lord is faithful; he will strengthen you and guard you from the evil one. (2 Thessalonians 3:3)

Chapter 28

REST

D o you feel, tired, uneasy, exhausted? Maybe it's time for a break. Take a break from your studies and other activities and relax. I know you have so much to do and you feel guilty about not focusing on your homework and other tasks, but everybody needs rest.

Getting rest for your body may be as easy as taking a "power nap," or getting to bed earlier tonight. Without proper rest, the human body will collapse. A shortage of sleep can suppress your immune system and increase your chances of getting sick. Studies have shown lack of sleep can also drastically affect your mind. It can affect your judgment, impair your memory, and even hinder your ability to learn. It can also alter your mood significantly. It causes irritability and anger and may lessen your ability to cope with stress. Lack of proper rest can even put you at greater risk for depression.

Rest is not always a physical thing. There is also a spiritual rest. That's when you feel peace and the anxiety of the day is lifted. God can provide you with both kinds of rest if you ask. The Bible tells you to give all your worries to Him because He cares for you. Jesus knew people throughout time would struggle with heavy burdens. He addressed this by telling you to come to him with your problems. If you do, He will help you with your burdens and give you rest.

When my kids were small, they wanted to be independent. Whenever we were travelling, they each had their own little suitcase. They would drag their suitcases as far as they could, then look into my eyes and say, "Daddy, can you carry it the rest of the way?" I always did. I did it because my heart was full of love for them. I was happy to take away their heavy load from them. So is your heavenly Father. Just ask Him.

My kids would often play all day and then collapse in my lap. Many times I carried them to bed, kissed their forehead and said a prayer over them. Your heavenly Father will do the same for you. He is always watching over you, and He knows when you've been working or playing too hard. He will help you find a peaceful rest as He holds you in his arms and gently rocks you to sleep. Don't resist. Whatever you are worrying about can wait. Spend time with God and He will give you rest. Study the scriptures below to understand more.

Say this prayer...

Lord, I'm tired. I've been studying really hard and I'm still behind. I have so many things to do! I can't do this on my own. I need you to help me carry this load. I can't get behind on things. I need you to help me work through all the deadlines, and responsibilities, so I will be successful, but still get some rest. I thank you Lord for your rest and your peace. Give me favor in my studies and with my teachers. Fill my life with peace and strength to make it through what's ahead. I ask this in Jesus' Name. Amen.

What does the Bible tell us?

Give all your worries and cares to God, for he cares about you. (1 Peter 5:7)

The Lord is my shepherd; I have all that I need. He lets me rest in green meadows; he leads me beside peaceful streams. He renews my strength. He guides me along right paths, bringing honor to his name. (Psalm 23:1-3)

Have you never heard? Have you never understood? The Lord is the everlasting God, the Creator of all the earth. He never grows weak or weary. No one can measure the depths of his under-standing. He gives power to the weak and strength to the pow-erless. Even youths will become weak and tired, and young men will fall in exhaustion. But those who trust in the Lord will find new strength. They will soar high on wings like eagles. They will run and not grow weary. They will walk and not faint. (Isaiah 40:28-31)

Then Jesus said, "Come to me, all of you who are weary and carry heavy burdens, and I will give you rest. Take my yoke upon you. Let me teach you, because I am humble and gentle at heart, and you will find rest for your souls. For my yoke is easy to bear, and the burden I give you is light." (Matthew 11:28-30)

This is what the Lord says: "Stop at the crossroads and look around. Ask for the old, godly way, and walk in it. Travel its path, and you will find rest for your souls. (Jeremiah 6:16)

...there is a special rest still waiting for the people of God. For all who have entered into God's rest have rested from their labors, just as God did after creating the world. So let us do our best to enter that rest... (Hebrews 4:9-10)

Chapter 29

SALVATION

Salvation is a fancy word that has become more associated with "religion" than its actual purpose. Some of you have heard it but don't really understand what it means. Let's make it simple. God wants to save you. What is He saving you from? Well, to put it simply, He wants to save you from the evils of this world and the next.

Yes, there is life after death. Some things are true whether you believe them or not. Society likes to believe in heaven because they envision a beautiful place. They like the idea of floating on a cloud with angels and walking on golden streets. Here's the catch. You can't receive what the Bible says about Heaven without accepting the reality of Hell.

People seem to fall into one of two camps. One group doesn't believe in Hell because they can't imagine God would allow such a place to exist. Others think Hell is a place where the "naughty" go. They expect to join their departed friends in a party that never ends. Well, they have one part right. It will never end. There is a thing called eternity, and we are all going to spend it somewhere. Heaven is a wonderful place where there are no tears, no pain, and you live in the presence of God himself. Hell is a place of weeping, darkness, fire, and gnashing of teeth. This is an easy choice isn't it?

That's the most important part. You have a choice. God gave us something called "free will." He didn't create robots to follow Him around and do His heavenly bidding. He created humans with emotions, and feelings, and the ability to make decisions on their own. Then He put a choice in front of you. Go to a wonderful place, or go to a horrible place. Even though He loves you, He will never force you one way or the other. He simply beckons you to come to Him. He wants you to experience the fullness of life on the earth, followed by an eternity with Him in Heaven.

How does this work? How do you get into heaven? Well, let's start with a quick bit of history. In the beginning, God created everything. Then He created some rules called "The Law." God was serious about this. If you broke the Law and sinned against Him, the penalty was death! Then, later God made a provision. When His followers broke the law, they were able to offer a sacrifice. In other words, instead of the sinner being killed, they were able to offer an animal in their place. If you are new to this it may sound weird, but that's how it worked. The reason it had to be an animal was because something had to die in their place. Blood had to be shed because of the person's disobedience. There had to be a "substitute" for the sinner. This process lasted for thousands of years.

Then God developed a new plan. This new plan was to send His own son to live with us as a human. His name was Jesus. When Jesus was on earth, he taught about God, and helped explain God's principles in a way people could understand. Then Jesus gave the ultimate sacrifice. He allowed himself to be crucified and die as the ultimate sacrifice for all mankind. When he died, he took your place. Because of his death, you can escape punishment for your sins. You simply ask for forgiveness in the name of Jesus.

So, how do you tap into this salvation and forgiveness of sins? For something this important, there must be a difficult test. Surely there must be an enormous final exam. Well, that's the best part. God made it simple. If you accept His Son (Jesus), and believe he died for your sins, then you can be saved. That is what salvation means.

Salvation is a multifaceted gift. First, it allows you to become part of God's family. Essentially, you are adopted into His family and have access to everything your new Father has to offer. Salvation also includes forgiveness of your sins. All you have to do is ask. As a bonus, God will provide you with a most amazing gift called eternal life. What does eternal life mean exactly? This means once your body dies here on earth, your spirit lives on. The part of you that makes you unique will live forever in Heaven. Some people call salvation "life" insurance. Others call it "fire" insurance. Either way, it's a policy you can't afford to ignore.

Maybe you are still skeptical. You've seen movies that make fun of Christians, or show a caricature of Christians as being "fake." You think it isn't "cool" to be religious, or conservative, or talk about God and stuff. I get it. Society rebels against anything with rules. They don't want to be held accountable for their own deeds. Some people would rather reject Jesus and fit in with the crowd, than accept Jesus and stand out. Don't let pride, stubbornness, or the "cool factor" keep you from the most important decision of your life. All you have to do is accept Jesus. Accept him for who he is and what he did for you. Read the Scriptures below to learn more about what he has done and will do for you. Then pray this prayer.

Say this prayer...

Dear God, I understand my sins have kept me separated from You. I also know You are the God of forgiveness. I want to turn away from my past life today. Jesus, I trust you and I want you to be my Lord and Savior. I believe you are the son of God, and you died for my sins. The Bible says you died as a sacrifice for my sins, but were resurrected and still live. I know you hear my prayers, so I commit my life into your hands. Help me to obey you and live a life that is pleasing to you. Thank you for saving me. I ask this in Jesus' Name. Amen.

What does the Bible tell us?

Jesus replied, "I tell you the truth, unless you are born again, you cannot see the Kingdom of God." (John 3:3)

For this is how God loved the world: He gave his one and only Son, so that everyone who believes in him will not perish but have eternal life. God sent his Son into the world not to judge the world, but to save the world through him. (John 3:16-17)

They replied, "Believe in the Lord Jesus and you will be saved, along with everyone in your household." (Acts 16:31)

And what do you benefit if you gain the whole world but lose your own soul? Is anything worth more than your soul? (Matthew 16:26)

If you openly declare that Jesus is Lord and believe in your heart that God raised him from the dead, you will be saved. For it is by believing in your heart that you are made right with God, and it is by openly declaring your faith that you are saved. (Romans 10:9-10)

But to all who believed him and accepted him, he gave the right to become children of God. (John 1:12)

God saved you by his grace when you believed. And you can't take credit for this; it is a gift from God. Salvation is not a reward for the good things we have done, so none of us can boast about it. (Ephesians 2:8-9)

Chapter 30

SELF-ESTEEM

We all question our self-worth from time to time. We wonder why we aren't more popular, better looking, or more talented. You may feel like you are nothing special and wonder about your place in the world. You got frustrated with yourself because you failed at something. Maybe someone embarrassed you when they laughed at your idea. You struggle with how to fit in.

You need to understand two important truths. First, everyone is different. We look different on the outside, and we are wired differently on the inside. Genetics play a part in the big picture. That's why you have your mom's nose, or your dad's eyes. Apart from that, you are a unique person with different dreams and a different personality.

Here is the second and most important truth. You are special to God. He made you! He's had the design plan for humans for a very long time. He could have easily made us the same, but He chose to make us different. Even identical twins have different personalities. Life would be boring if everyone looked and thought alike. God gave you a unique brain and threw in quirks and hidden talents to make it interesting. You may not feel special, but you are.

Unfortunately, society seems fascinated with extremes. They only show the skinniest models in magazines and only talk about the fastest athletes. If you compare yourself against these extremes, you may feel inadequate. Don't fall into that trap. These are not the norms. The human race contains billions of humans and we're all different. Don't be so hard on yourself. Each of us is good (and bad) at different things. You may struggle to see your own positive attributes. Ask a friend what they like about you. You'll be surprised at the wonderful things others see in you. Don't focus on comparison with others. Rejoice in how amazing God made you. There is nobody on earth like you.

The hardest impact to your self-esteem often comes from others. Maybe you were bullied in school and those hurtful words keep coming back to you. Maybe someone said harsh words that left you feeling worthless or somehow inferior. This may have even come from someone close to you. This can get to you. I understand. Words can hurt so much. Let God heal those scars. Ask Him.

Each of us struggle with people's opinions, our own perception of ourselves, and God's opinion of us. While each of these is important, God's opinion is the only accurate one. God created you and loves you more than you can imagine. God accepts you as you are, with your flaws, shortcomings, and sins. God doesn't look at what you *can't* do; He looks at what you *can* do. While society often focuses on our physical attributes or skills, God only looks at the heart.

While this is an exciting time in your life, you are still trying to find your place in the world. You have so many wonderful years ahead, but you may feel inadequate. I have great news for you. God has a plan for your life. You have a specific place in this world because you are a unique person. God loves you and you are worthy of His plan. You are worthy of His love. Your past doesn't matter to Him. He's interested in your future! As a Christian, you are one of God's children. God doesn't watch over "some" of His children. Trust me... He has a special plan for you.

If you are dealing with low self-esteem, read the Scriptures below to find out what God says about you and who you are in Christ. No other opinion matters, including your own. God places great value on you. He created you in your mother's womb. He sent His Son to die for your sins. He has a place for you in this world. You were created in God's image. Start acting like it! Hold your head with confidence and set boundaries so people will treat you with dignity. You deserve respect like anyone else. As you live for God, you will find strength, hope, and new meaning for your life. As God heals your self-esteem, reach out and show love to others who may feel rejected.

Say this prayer...

Dear God, sometimes I feel so inadequate. It seems like I can't do what others can do. I'm not as smart or athletic, or as beautiful as my friends. People have said hurtful things that I can't seem to let go. Help me forgive them, forget those words, and bring healing into my life. I want to feel confident about myself. I'm a unique person. There is nobody in the world like me and that makes me special to God. Help strengthen my self-worth, and give me confidence to stand up for myself. Take away the fear I have of others' opinions. Help me to feel Your love even when I don't feel it from others. I'm ready for a positive change in my life. Help me to see myself the way You see me. I ask this in Jesus' Name. Amen.

What does the Bible tell us?

...The Lord doesn't see things the way you see them. People judge by outward appearance, but the Lord looks at the heart." (1 Samuel 16:7)

Obviously, I'm not trying to win the approval of people, but of God. If pleasing people were my goal, I would not be Christ's servant. (Galatians 1:10)

Thank you for making me so wonderfully complex! Your workmanship is marvelous—how well I know it. (Psalm 139:14)

So God created human beings in his own image. In the image of God he created them; male and female he created them. (Genesis 1:27)

Give all your worries and cares to God, for he cares about you. (1 Peter 5:7)

...those the Father has given me will come to me, and I will never reject them. (John 6:37)

Can anything ever separate us from Christ's love? Does it mean he no longer loves us if we have trouble or calamity, or are persecuted, or hungry, or destitute, or in danger, or threatened with death? ; No, despite all these things, overwhelming victory is ours through Christ, who loved us. And I am convinced that nothing can ever separate us from God's love. Neither death nor life, neither angels nor demons, neither our fears for today nor our worries about tomorrow—not even the powers of hell can separate us from God's love. No power in the sky above or in the earth below—indeed, nothing in all creation will ever be able to separate us from the love of God that is revealed in Christ Jesus our Lord. (Romans 8:35, 37-39)

Chapter 31

SEX

Genesis tells us that Eve was made for Adam. Every man and woman created since has been made in the same image. As we explore this further, we need to have a candid discussion about sex. Forgive me if this makes you uncomfortable, but it is important that we talk frankly. As young adults, it is essential that you understand the truth about sex.

Biology shows that men and women were made for each other. We learned this in junior high health class. Men and women have different anatomies, but they complement each other. Our reproductive organs fit together in a way to allow conception. Based on our divine design, it is obvious that sex was intended for procreation. In other words, men and women having sex is part of God's plan. God wanted to populate the earth, so He made men and women attractive to one another. God also wanted us to enjoy sex, so He made it pleasurable. From God's perspective, there is no guilt in the sexual act. It is meant to be intimate and private, but sex was never meant to be "bad." There is one "catch" though; God designed all of this for you and your spouse.

It's true. Sex was intended for a husband and wife. It was designed as one of the wonderful benefits of marriage. When you make a lifelong commitment to a person, you share everything including your bodies. Under this blessed union, you have the ability to create life through God's miraculous process.

The trouble is mankind is by nature, rebellious. We don't like rules, and we don't like to be told what to do. We ignore God's rules around marriage, and decide to have sex with whomever we choose. This creates many, many problems such as sexual impurity, adultery, diseases, unwanted pregnancies, and many other issues that are not part of God's plan.

It seems each generation has a more casual attitude towards sex than the one before, but this doesn't mean it is right in God's eyes. Nowadays people talk about "hooking up," "one night stands," and even "friends with benefits." The sad truth is that all of these situations go directly against God's wishes for your life. I know this may not be the popular message in this day of relaxed attitudes about sex, but there is only one Truth. God's rules were created to protect you and allow you to fulfill the plan He has for your life.

When you break God's rules, you are interfering with His best for you. God is not a taskmaster with a whip forcing you to follow His rules. He is not trying to fence you in. He is building a fence to keep out the enemy. God is your protector. You need to follow the rules of His kingdom and not wander outside the gate. God is a loving counselor, providing direction and guidance to keep you on a safe path that leads away from danger and towards His blessings. He tries to guide us away from temptation, but we rebel.

We react like a child throwing a temper tantrum when the parent takes away something unsafe.

When my kids were young, they liked to explore. Sometimes they found something sharp, or hot, or somehow dangerous. As a good father, I took it away from them, or led them away from the danger. I knew it was for their safety, but they didn't always like it. They wanted to play with the shiny scissors, or put their fingers near the fireplace. They didn't want my rules. As adults, we rebel in the same way when our heavenly Father tells us "No!"

The Bible is the living Word of God. God's viewpoint on sex is very clear in the Bible. His message is just as relative today as it was thousands of years ago. Look at the Scriptures below and you will understand what God expects from you.

Say this prayer...

(If you have already had sex)
Lord, I messed up. I had sex and I'm not married. I didn't really think it was a big deal. Everyone seems to be doing it. I was just trying to fit in and I wanted people to like me. Now I know it was wrong. I'm ashamed of some things I did. I can't get those memories to go away. I ask for your forgiveness. A few people know what I did, and I'm embarrassed when I see them. Take away the guilt, the shame, and the burden of my past. Help me to move forward in wholeness and keep myself pure from now on. With your help, I want to start fresh and follow Your advice. I ask this in Jesus' Name. Amen.

(If you are still a virgin)
Lord, it's been difficult, but I'm still a virgin. Most people don't know because these days it's embarrassing. I don't want people to think I'm a prude. I don't want anyone to

think I'm weird. I believe in Your word. It tells me that sex is for marriage. I really want to save myself for marriage. It may not be popular, but it's Biblical. Help me to remain pure. Help keep me out of intimate situations that would tempt me to sin. Give me the self-control to save myself for my wedding night. I ask this in Jesus' Name. Amen.

What does the Bible tell us?

Because we belong to the day, we must live decent lives for all to see. Don't participate in the darkness of wild parties and drunkenness, or in sexual promiscuity and immoral living, or in quarreling and jealousy. Instead, clothe yourself with the presence of the Lord Jesus Christ. And don't let yourself think about ways to indulge your evil desires. (Romans 13:13)

When you follow the desires of your sinful nature, the results are very clear: sexual immorality, impurity, lustful pleasures, idolatry, sorcery, hostility, quarreling, jealousy, outbursts of anger, selfish ambition, dissension, division, envy, drunkenness, wild parties, and other sins like these. Let me tell you again, as I have before, that anyone living that sort of life will not inherit the Kingdom of God. (Galatians 5:19-21)

Don't let anyone think less of you because you are young. Be an example to all believers in what you say, in the way you live, in your love, your faith, and your purity. (1 Timothy 4:12)

How can a young person stay pure? By obeying your word. (Psalm 119:9)

Run from anything that stimulates youthful lusts. Instead, pursue righteous living, faithfulness, love, and peace. Enjoy the companionship of those who call on the Lord with pure hearts. *(2 Timothy 2:22)*

So put to death the sinful, earthly things lurking within you. Have nothing to do with sexual immorality, impurity, lust, and evil desires. Don't be greedy, for a greedy person is an idolater, worshiping the things of this world. (Colossians 3:5)

Run from sexual sin! No other sin so clearly affects the body as this one does. For sexual immorality is a sin against your own body. Don't you realize that your body is the temple of the Holy Spirit, who lives in you and was given to you by God? You do not belong to yourself, 20 for God bought you with a high price. So you must honor God with your body. (1 Corinthians 6:18-20)

Chapter 32

SUICIDE

It's sad that I even need to include this chapter. Unfortunately, the statistics of young people committing suicide continues to rise. The amount of pressure placed on us by society continues to increase. The need to "fit in" starts in elementary school. There are cliques like the jocks, the band kids, drama kids, mean girls, the popular kids, and you name it. Outside of school (and sometimes inside), gangs are always available to lure new members. Even though there are anti-bully campaigns, we know they are still around making kid's lives miserable. One thing is consistent, young people are always looking for someone to accept them.

Looks and fashion dominate the media. You can't be too small, too tall, too heavy, too thin. You must wear the right clothes, have the right haircut, listen to the right music, and drive the right car. The competition for many things in society has increased and it's the same with college. It's getting harder to make it into the "good" schools. There is so much pressure to maintain your grades. It can become a bit overwhelming.

Let me tell you a secret. What really matters is what's in your heart. God loves you for who you are. He will meet you wherever you are. He loves the shy, the outgoing, the handsome, the plain, the uncoordinated, the athletic, and the ones nobody ever notices. He loves you and wants to develop a relationship with you. Don't worry about what society says you must do. Find out what the Lord wants from you. The Bible provides all the answers you need.

Maybe your sadness comes from a different place. Perhaps your parents weren't good role models. God says He will be your Father! Maybe you did something awful and you can't forgive yourself. God can forgive you! You can share your most shocking secrets with Him and He won't even flinch. There is nothing God hasn't seen or heard before. Maybe you've been through a lifetime of disappointments. Maybe the person you loved didn't return your affection. Maybe you've simply lost hope.

I have some really good news. God is the God of hope. God holds your future in His hands. If you give your life to Christ, and give your troubles to him, he will bring you out of your desperation. Suicide is never the answer. Suicide is just a trick of the devil. He is a master at confusion. He convinces people there is nothing to live for. He wants to take away your future. If you commit suicide, he succeeds. Don't listen to him. You are smarter than that! Satan will even trick you into believing he doesn't exist and it's all in your mind. God is real, but you need to understand the devil is real too. He will try to take you to a dark place. God is much more powerful. If you reach out to God, He will always defeat the devil.

The Bible tells us Satan is the father of lies. He will say that you aren't pretty or handsome enough, you don't have any talent, and nobody loves you. He whispers these thoughts to you repeatedly to make you think the world would be better without you. Don't fall for it! These are all lies. How do we know? We know because he is the father of lies! This is what he does for a living! His job is to steal, kill, and destroy. He wants to hurt anything good. He will try to steal your confidence, kill your dreams, and destroy your self-esteem.

Have you ever seen the movie "It's a wonderful life?" The main character is despondent and wishes he had never been born. Then an angel shows him the ripple effect of how many people would be impacted negatively if he had never existed. God really does have a plan for your life. Your life will impact many others. You just can't see it right now. Trust God. Tell Him how you feel, and give your life to Him. He can take away your sadness, frustration and turn your life around.

The Bible says God has a plan for everyone, so I know God has a plan for you! Give Him a chance to help you succeed as you walk hand in hand into your future. God loves you. He is watching you right now. Talk to Him. You can tell him all about your situation and He will listen. God says so in His Word and He never lies. Say the prayer below, and then look at the Scriptures under the prayer. You'll see how special you are to Him.

Say this prayer...

Lord, I'm so tired. I don't feel like going on. I feel so alone, but the Scriptures below say You are listening to me. If You are listening, I need Your help. Give me hope. Give me joy and happiness. Restore the sparkle to my eyes and help me to dream again. My heart is broken, but I know You can heal my broken heart. Rescue me from this deep hole I'm in. The Bible says nothing can separate me from Your love. So, show me Your love. Make it real to me. I have a choice between life and death, and I choose life. I choose to live but I need Your help. Forgive me for my past sins, wash away all the bad things that have happened to me, and help me not to listen to all the negative thoughts. The Bible says I have the mind of Christ. It also says You are not the author of confusion. So I just pray against any negative or confusing thoughts. I confess that my mind will be clear and I will have a positive outlook. Now that I know You are my heavenly Father, I know You are watching over me. I realize You love me and I am valuable in Your eyes. Thank you for saving me. I ask this in Jesus' Name. Amen.

If you need help, please call the National Suicide Prevention Hotline: 1-800-273-0255.

Or contact them online: www.suicidepreventionlifeline.org (Live Chat is available)

What does the Bible tell us?

The Lord hears his people when they call to him for help. He rescues them from all their troubles. The Lord is close to the brokenhearted; he rescues those whose spirits are crushed. The righteous person faces many troubles, but the Lord comes to the rescue each time. (Psalm 34:17-19)

For I know the plans I have for you," says the Lord. "They are plans for good and not for disaster, to give you a future and a hope. (Jeremiah 29:11)

And I am convinced that nothing can ever separate us from God's love. Neither death nor life, neither angels nor demons, neither our fears for today nor our worries about tomorrow—not even the powers of hell can separate us from God's love. No power in the sky above or in the earth below—indeed, nothing in all creation will ever be able to separate us from the love of God that is revealed in Christ Jesus our Lord. (Romans 8:38)

Don't be a fool! Why die before your time? (Ecclesiastes 7:17)

He heals the brokenhearted and bandages their wounds. (Psalm 147:3)

"Don't let your hearts be troubled. Trust in God, and trust also in me. (John 14:1)

"Today I have given you the choice between life and death, between blessings and curses. Now I call on heaven and earth to witness the choice you make. Oh, that you would choose life, so that you and your descendants might live! You can make this choice by loving the Lord your God, obeying him, and committing yourself firmly to him. This is the key to your life... (Deuteronomy 30:19-20)

Chapter 33

TEMPTATION

What is temptation exactly? It brings to mind a strange combination of good and evil. It focuses on something that seems desirable, but you know you shouldn't. To be more specific, temptation is the lure, attraction, or seduction to something typically considered *bad*, or at least bad *for* you. It is a craving for something. Temptation comes in many forms: money, sex, power, and even dessert.

While we may be tempted to have a second slice of cheesecake, let's focus on the more serious temptations to sin against God. Satan has been in the business of luring us into sin since the beginning of time. It started a long time ago when Eve was lured into eating the forbidden fruit in Genesis 3:4-6. God gave Adam and Eve instructions that included not eating the fruit of a certain tree. Then Satan convinced Eve that God didn't really mean it. He pulled on her desire to have the forbidden fruit, and on her desire to be like God. Her lack of self-control caused her to cross a line God had drawn, and there were consequences to all mankind.

How does Satan do it? He uses your flesh. We already have natural desires for food, success, sex, to be loved, to be powerful. He manipulates us by using our own minds and bodies against us. He uses your physical senses (sight, hearing, smell, touch, taste). Those five alone can get you into a lot of trouble. The trick is to be strong and have the self-control needed to ignore the temptation and stand firm. God tells us to *"Keep watch and pray, so that you will not give in to temptation. For the spirit is willing, but the body is weak!"(Matthew 26:41)*. This is a battle between your mind and your body. Your body craves certain physical things like an addict craves a drug.

While some temptations are related to your physical body, many temptations are related to your mind. Your mind is tempted with things like power, money, and gossip. You may be tempted to do something, or say something unethical to gain an advantage on the competition. You may be tempted to manipulate others to improve your own position. The pull of temptation in these situations can be just as powerful as the physical. Again, self-control is the only answer.

Society has adapted a motto of "If it feels good, do it." The Bible tells us something different. It tells us not everything that *seems* good is good *for* you. Things that "feel" good are not always beneficial. Cheesecake can be wonderful, but those unwanted pounds are a direct side effect. In a more serious example, pre-marital sex can lead to an unplanned pregnancy. When it comes to temptation, we often ignore the consequences for a moment of bliss.

If you are dealing with temptation, don't be too hard on yourself. It happens to everyone. Don't let Satan suggest you are a bad person. Everyone struggles with temptation from time to time. In fact, when Jesus taught his disciples how to pray in the famous "Lord's prayer" (Mathew 6:9-13), he told the disciples to pray that they wouldn't yield to temptation. He knew it would happen to even those closest to him.

Know this. God does <u>not</u> tempt you. He will not allow temptation to be more than you can handle (1 Corinthians 10:13). This means that no matter how enticing the temptation is, you are strong enough to overcome it with God's help. Keep reading to find out more.

Say this prayer...

Lord, help me not to give in to temptation. I have good intentions, but I feel drawn to things I shouldn't be doing. Sometimes I'm drawn to people who are a bad influence on me. Give me strength, give me wisdom, and help me with my self-control. I want to succeed in life but don't want to take unethical measures to get there. I want to live a life that is holy and pure so I will please You. I ask this in Jesus' Name. Amen.

What does the Bible tell us?

For the world offers only a craving for physical pleasure, a craving for everything we see, and pride in our achievements and posses-sions. These are not from the Father, but are from this world. (1 John 2:16)

And remember, when you are being tempted, do not say, "God is tempting me." God is never tempted to do wrong, and he never tempts anyone else. Temptation comes from our own desires, which entice us and drag us away. These desires give birth to sinful actions. And when sin is allowed to grow, it gives birth to death. (James 1:13-15)

The temptations in your life are no different from what others experience. And God is faithful. He will not allow the temptation to be more than you can stand. When you are tempted, he will show you a way out so that you can endure. (1 Corinthians 10:13)

And don't let us yield to temptation, but rescue us from the evil one. (Matthew 6:13)

God blesses those who patiently endure testing and temptation. Afterward they will receive the crown of life that God has promised to those who love him. (James 1:12)

Temptation comes from our own desires, which entice us and drag us away. (James 1:14)

Keep watch and pray, so that you will not give in to temptation. For the spirit is willing, but the body is weak!" (Matthew 26:41)

Chapter 34

YOUR FUTURE

D o you look to your future with excitement and hope? Or do you view the future with anxiousness and fear? What changes your perspective? If you develop a basic plan for your life, it reduces the anxiety of the unknown and points you in the right direction. The trick is looking into your future and planning your first steps.

Have you ever seen a beginning puzzle for a toddler? It is usually only a few large rigid pieces and the pieces all fit inside a frame. The frame shows a bit of the picture, so it is easier to see where the pieces go. For some of you, life is like this. You have a basic idea of where things will fit, and you just need to work out the details. If you are in this group, the future can be an exciting time full of adventure.

For others, life resembles one of those 3D "stereogram" pictures. Those pictures that look like nonsense, but you stare at it hoping the mystery picture will appear. For some, the hidden picture pops into focus quickly. For others you continue to stare but see nothing. Similarly, the future seems to come into focus quickly for some but not for others. That blurry, hazy view of the future can seem dark, ominous, and frustrating. Like those confusing pictures, your glimpse into a vague future can bring uneasiness.

None of us really knows what will happen. We put together plans, hopes, and dreams, and we head out in that direction. Unfortunately, life has a way of dropping obstacles in your path. The dream job you envisioned isn't available in the town you expected. The person you fell in love with has a job offer in another town. These surprises and twists make life interesting, but also scary. I look back at my life and I'm amazed how I got here. Many events shaped my life that I could not have predicted. You can't predict your own future.

Often you get hints about your future. These thoughts wait quietly under the surface like a friendly suggestion in the back of your mind. For my wife it was art. She always enjoyed drawing and had the basic skills. She chose a different path and graduated with an electrical engineering degree, but later in life became a portrait artist. For me it was writing. Did I expect to be an author? No. Years ago a teacher gave me an "A+" on an assignment I wrote for English class. She wrote a little note on my paper to tell me it was good. Her comments stayed with me. Throughout my life, I've always had a knack for communicating complicated things in simple way. While I decided to pursue engineering and a more technical path, this other gifting remained in the back of my mind. Later I felt God urging me to encourage others through writing. That high school memory was there encouraging me when I wrote my first newspaper column. It was there when I wrote my first book, and it is still here as I write this book. I was only a teenager, but that teacher's encouragement gave me hope and a good feeling about my future. What encouraging words have you heard? What do you feel in your heart? Ask God to reveal those things. They could turn into a hobby or even a career.

Maybe you've never had anyone to encourage you. You may have no idea what you want to do with your life. Maybe you are even questioning your college major. It's OK. Everyone is different. You aren't "behind" or "late" on your plans. Let me encourage you with this. God can help. If you seek God about your future, there is no reason to worry. It's going to work out. Take the burden off your shoulders and give it to God to work out. He has a plan for your life. I know because He has a plan for everyone.

I hope these words give you comfort, and a peace concerning your future. I know many different students will read this book. You will be from different majors, cultures, countries, and unique circumstances. You may have been worried about the future. Now you know you can be extremely confident in your future. One thing remains supernaturally consistent. The Bible says God has plans for you. *"They are plans for good and not for disaster, to give you a future and a hope."* Look to your future with hope, and excitement because God has great things in store for you. Look at the words of encouragement He provides in the scriptures below.

Say this prayer...

Lord, give me peace about my future. I want to be excited, but I'm nervous. I want great things for my future, and I want my dreams to come true. You know everything Lord. You know what is inside my heart. Help me to make the right decisions. Open the right doors for me so I can be everything You want me to be. Help me to be prepared. Give me guidance, support, and protection as I step into the unknown. I know You will be with me Father, because the Bible says You will never leave us. *Thank you for loving me enough to watch over my future. Help me to listen to Your voice and keep me on the right path. I ask this in Jesus' Name. Amen.*

What does the Bible tell us?

For I know the plans I have for you," says the Lord. "They are plans for good and not for disaster, to give you a future and a hope. (Jeremiah 29:11)

The Lord says, "I will guide you along the best pathway for your life. I will advise you and watch over you. (Psalm 32:8)

You guide me with your counsel, leading me to a glorious destiny. (Psalm 73:24)

For I can do everything through Christ, who gives me strength. (Philippians 4:13)

Trust in the Lord with all your heart; do not depend on your own understanding. Seek his will in all you do, and he will show you which path to take. (Proverbs 3:5-6)

Guard your heart above all else, for it determines the course of your life. (Proverbs 4:23)

This is my command—be strong and courageous! Do not be afraid or discouraged. For the Lord your God is with you wherever you go." (Joshua 1:9)

Chapter 35

WISDOM

Wisdom. This may seem like an odd topic for a book directed at college students. You have already chosen to further your education by learning all you can about your planned profession. You are studying hard and doing your best to succeed. While education focuses on memorizing facts and formulas, true wisdom goes beyond that. Knowledge is about gathering information, but wisdom is knowing how and when to apply this knowledge. We're not just talking about school. We're talking about life!

The Bible states that Solomon was the wisest man who ever lived. However, he wasn't always. He asked God for wisdom. He said, *"Give me an understanding heart so that I can govern your people well and know the difference between right and wrong." (1 Kings 3:9)* The Scripture also states God was pleased Solomon had asked for wisdom instead of wealth, or long life, or the death of his enemies.

What could be more valuable than knowing "what" to do and "when" to do it? Throughout your college years, you will make decisions with insufficient information. It may be as simple as which course to choose. It could be which career to pursue. It could be deciding whether the person you are attracted to is the right one for you. Wouldn't it be great to have a partner in all those decisions? The Bible says, *"fear of the Lord is the foundation of true wisdom."* *(Psalm 111:10)* Following His directions will lead to wise choices. The Scriptures even reveal Wisdom will add years to your life! (*Proverbs 9:11*) When you ask God for wisdom, you are also giving Him the right to step into your life and provide direction. Only He knows the future, so wouldn't it be great to get the inside scoop?

When my son was born, I prayed God would watch over him all the days of his life and give him what he needed to succeed. I had one of those *"Lion King"* moments where I raised his tiny body into the moonlight and asked God to bless him with wisdom. Is it a coincidence that he became a National Merit Scholar and has five wisdom teeth? Maybe, but it seems like a little wink from God to let me know He was listening. It makes me smile. Did I do everything right as a Father? Of course not... but I did ask the most powerful person in the universe to bless my son with a very important gift.

Like Solomon, when you ask for wisdom you are surpassing all the worldly treasures like money and fame in favor of a gift that will help you and others. Some say education is the key to a successful future. I suggest God's wisdom is the key to all things, present and future. Proverbs 8:1-2 states *"wisdom calls out"* and *"takes her stand at the crossroads."* We need wisdom the most when we are standing at the crossroads of life and need direction. God is waiting for you to ask for wisdom as you stand at your own crossroads. Say the prayer below and review the Scriptures provided.

Say this prayer...

Lord, I ask for wisdom. I still struggle with many decisions and I'm not sure about the future. I need your help. I'm doing the things I know to keep moving forward, but I see many crossroads. Help me to make the right decisions...to know right from wrong. Give me an understanding heart when dealing with life, and provide counsel and direction when dealing with others. I ask this in Jesus' Name. Amen.

What does the Bible tell us?

If you need wisdom, ask our generous God, and he will give it to you. He will not rebuke you for asking. (James 1:5)

Fear of the Lord is the foundation of wisdom. Knowledge of the Holy One results in good judgment. Wisdom will multiply your days and add years to your life. If you become wise, you will be the one to benefit. If you scorn wisdom, you will be the one to suffer. (Proverbs 9:10-12)

In the same way, wisdom is sweet to your soul. If you find it, you will have a bright future, and your hopes will not be cut short. (Proverbs 24:14)

Tune your ears to wisdom, and concentrate on understanding. Cry out for insight, and ask for understanding. Search for them as you would for silver; seek them like hidden treasures. Then you will understand what it means to fear the Lord, and you will gain knowledge of God. For the Lord grants wisdom! From his mouth come knowledge and understanding. He grants a treasure of common sense to the honest. He is a shield to those who walk with integrity. He guards the paths of the just and protects those who are faithful to him. Then you will understand what is right, just, and fair, and you will find the right way to go. For wisdom will enter your heart, and knowledge will fill you with joy. Wise choices will watch over you. Understanding will keep you safe. Wisdom will save you from evil people, from those whose words are twisted. (Proverbs 2: 2-12)

Joyful is the person who finds wisdom, the one who gains understanding. For wisdom is more profitable than silver, and her wages are better than gold. Wisdom is more precious than rubies; nothing you desire can compare with her. She offers you long life in her right hand, and riches and honor in her left. She will guide you down delightful paths; all her ways are satisfying. Wisdom is a tree of life to those who embrace her; happy are those who hold her tightly. (Proverbs 3:13-18)

Get all the advice and instruction you can, so you will be wise the rest of your life. (Proverbs 19:20)

Trust in the Lord with all your heart; do not depend on your own understanding. Seek his will in all you do, and he will show you which path to take. (Proverbs 3:5-6)

FINAL THOUGHTS

As I close, I want to leave you with some parting comments. Don't be overwhelmed by this unique time in your life. Cherish your college years. You will look back on these years as some of the most fun times ever. While schoolwork is challenging, the real trials begin after graduation as you step into your new job, future families, and additional responsibilities. Use this book. The Scriptures included will speak to you during and after college. God's word is the same *yesterday, today and forever*.

The key to success in your life is an intimate relationship with God. Don't wait until something bad happens to search for Him. Be proactive. Talk to Him every day and ask for His advice. The Bible says, *"Trust in the Lord with all your heart; do not depend on your own understanding. Seek his will in all you do, and he will show you which path to take." (Proverbs 3:5-6)* There is no better advice.

Here is another great Scripture for students: *"Don't let the excitement of youth cause you to forget your Creator. Honor him in your youth before you grow old..." (Ecclesiastes 12:1)* Young adults are often busy with fun and friends and forget about God. Don't let this happen to you. He is your divine Counselor. Make sure He's involved in all your decisions.

Finally, don't forget those loved ones who helped you get to where you are. Most of you have parents, friends, grandparents, uncles, and aunts who love you and want the best for you. Some of them have been financially responsible for your tuition, food, and even the clothes on your back. They have also given you encouragement and emotional support. Maybe they haven't done everything right, but they are trying. If you haven't called them lately, give them a call and say thanks. When the whole world seems against you, there are people back home who love you.

If you simply seek God with all your heart, you will find Him, and He will take care of you. If you follow his Word, and treat others with respect, you will be successful and build many wonderful relationships.

I pray this book has helped you understand God's promises for you. God's Word is powerful. He truly has an answer for everything and a plan for your life.

Blessings,
Steve

CONTACT THE AUTHOR

I f this book has helped you in any way, I would love to hear from you. Please contact me through either of the methods below.

Web Address: www.StevanWilliamson.com

Mailing Address:

Stevan Williamson
P.O. Box 741906
Houston, TX 77274

Please include your questions, prayer requests, testimonies, and contact information when you write. I am also available for speaking engagements at your school, church, or other organization.

APPENDIX

Chapter 1: Anger

And "don't sin by letting anger control you." Don't let the sun go down while you are still angry, for anger gives a foothold to the devil. (Ephesians 4:26)

Get rid of all bitterness, rage, anger, harsh words, and slander, as well as all types of evil behavior. Instead, be kind to each other, tenderhearted, forgiving one another, just as God through Christ has forgiven you. (Ephesians 4:31-32)

Don't befriend angry people or associate with hot-tempered people, or you will learn to be like them and endanger your soul. (Proverbs 22:24-25)

A gentle answer deflects anger, but harsh words make tempers flare. (Proverbs 15:1)

An angry person starts fights; a hot-tempered person commits all kinds of sin. (Proverbs 29:22)

Hot-tempered people must pay the penalty. If you rescue them once, you will have to do it again. (Proverbs 19:19)

Sensible people control their temper; they earn respect by over-looking wrongs. (Proverbs 19:11)

A hot-tempered person starts fights; a cool-tempered person stops them. (Proverbs 15:18)

Stop being angry! Turn from your rage! Do not lose your temper—it only leads to harm. (Psalm 37:8)

Chapter 2: Anxiety/Stress

Can all your worries add a single moment to your life? And if worry can't accomplish a little thing like that, what's the use of worrying over bigger things? "Look at the lilies and how they grow. They don't work or make their clothing, yet Solomon in all his glory was not dressed as beautifully as they are. And if God cares so wonderfully for flowers that are here today and thrown into the fire tomorrow, he will certainly care for you. Why do you have so little faith? "And don't be concerned about what to eat and what to drink. Don't worry about such things. These things dominate the thoughts of unbelievers all over the world, but your Father already knows your needs. Seek the Kingdom of God above all else, and he will give you everything you need. (Luke 12:25-31)

Jesus said, "That is why I tell you not to worry about everyday life— whether you have enough food to eat or enough clothes to wear. For life is more than food, and your body more than clothing. Look at the ravens. They don't plant or harvest or store food in barns, for God feeds them. And you are far more valuable to him than any birds! (Luke 12:22-24)

When doubts filled my mind, your comfort gave me renewed hope and cheer. (Psalm 94:19)

It is useless for you to work so hard from early morning until late at night, anxiously working for food to eat; for God gives rest to his loved ones. (Psalm 127:2)

"Don't let your hearts be troubled. Trust in God, and trust also in me. (John 14:1)

In my distress I prayed to the LORD, and the LORD answered me and set me free. The LORD is for me, so I will have no fear. What can mere people do to me? Yes, the LORD is for me; he will help me. (Psalm 118:5-7)

As pressure and stress bear down on me, I find joy in your commands. (Psalms 119:143)

Chapter 3: Dating

Run from sexual sin! No other sin so clearly affects the body as this one does. For sexual immorality is a sin against your own body. (1 Corinthians 6:18)

Love is patient and kind. Love is not jealous or boastful or proud or rude. It does not demand its own way. It is not irritable, and it keeps no record of being wronged. It does not rejoice about injustice but rejoices whenever the truth wins out. Love never gives up, never loses faith, is always hopeful, and endures through every circumstance. (1 Corinthians 13:4-7)

Run from anything that stimulates youthful lusts. Instead, pursue righteous living, faithfulness, love, and peace. Enjoy the companionship of those who call on the Lord with pure hearts. (2 Timothy 2:22)

And all who have this eager expectation will keep themselves pure, just as he is pure. (1 John 3:3)

Chapter 4: Decisions

You can make many plans, but the Lord's purpose will prevail. (Proverbs 19:21)

If you are wise and understand God's ways, prove it by living an honorable life, doing good works with the humility that comes from wisdom. (James 3:13)

And we know that God causes everything to work together for the good of those who love God and are called according to his purpose for them. (Romans 8:28)

Chapter 5: Depression

And I am convinced that nothing can ever separate us from God's love. Neither death nor life, neither angels nor demons, neither our fears for today nor our worries about tomorrow—not even the powers of hell can separate us from God's love. No power in the sky above or in the earth below—indeed, nothing in all creation will ever be able to separate us from the love of God that is revealed in Christ Jesus our Lord. (Romans 8:38-39)

Then Jesus said, "Come to me, all of you who are weary and carry heavy burdens, and I will give you rest. Take my yoke upon you. Let me teach you, because I am humble and gentle at heart, and you will find rest for your souls. (Matthew 11:28-29)

Each time he said, "My grace is all you need. My power works best in weakness..". (2 Corinthians 12:9)

Come quickly, Lord, and answer me, for my depression deepens. Don't turn away from me, or I will die. Let me hear of your unfailing love each morning, for I am trusting you. Show me where to walk, for I give myself to you. Rescue me from my enemies, Lord; I run to you to hide me. Teach me to do your will, for you are my God. May your gracious Spirit lead me forward on a firm footing. For the glory of your name, O Lord, preserve my life. Because of your faithfulness, bring me out of this distress. (Psalm 143:7-11)

But you, O Lord, are a shield around me; you are my glory, the one who holds my head high. (Psalm 3:3)

Do not be afraid or discouraged, for the Lord will personally go ahead of you. He will be with you; he will neither fail you nor abandon you." (Deuteronomy 31:8)

Don't be afraid, for I am with you. Don't be discouraged, for I am your God. I will strengthen you and help you... (Isaiah 41:10)

When doubts filled my mind, your comfort gave me renewed hope and cheer. (Psalm 94:19)

Why am I discouraged? Why is my heart so sad? I will put my hope in God! I will praise him again—my Savior and my God! (Psalm 42:11)

Chapter 6: Drinking

But you must be careful so that your freedom does not cause others with a weaker conscience to stumble. (1 Corinthians 8:9)

Who has bloodshot eyes? It is the one who spends long hours in the taverns, trying out new drinks. Don't gaze at the wine, seeing how red it is, how it sparkles in the cup, how smoothly it goes down. For in the end it bites like a poisonous snake; it stings like a viper. You will see hallucinations, and you will say crazy things... (Proverbs 23:29-34)

Wine produces mockers; alcohol leads to brawls. Those led astray by drink cannot be wise. (Proverbs 20:1)

Chapter 7: Drugs

You have had enough in the past of the evil things that godless people enjoy—their immorality and lust, their feasting and drunkenness and wild parties... Of course, your former friends are surprised when you no longer plunge into the flood of wild and destructive things they do. So they slander you. But remember that they will have to face God, who stands ready to judge everyone, both the living and the dead. (1 Peter 4:3-5)

I plead with you to give your bodies to God because of all he has done for you. Let them be a living and holy sacrifice—the kind he will find acceptable. (Romans 12:1)

Chapter 8: Eating Disorders

Keep watch and pray, so that you will not give in to temptation. For the spirit is willing, but the body is weak." (Mark 14:38)

But in my distress I cried out to the Lord; yes, I prayed to my God for help. He heard me from his sanctuary; my cry to him reached his ears. (Psalm 18:6)

He lifted me out of the pit of despair, out of the mud and the mire. He set my feet on solid ground and steadied me as I walked along. (Psalm 40:2)

I prayed to the Lord, and he answered me. He freed me from all my fears. (Psalms 34:4)

Since he himself has gone through suffering and testing, he is able to help us when we are being tested. (Hebrews 2:18)

For the Kingdom of God is not a matter of what we eat or drink, but of living a life of goodness and peace and joy in the Holy Spirit. (Romans 14:17)

Confess your sins to each other and pray for each other so that you may be healed. The earnest prayer of a righteous person has great power and produces wonderful results. (James 5:16)

Chapter 9: Employment

But you are not controlled by your sinful nature. You are controlled by the Spirit if you have the Spirit of God living in you. (And remember that those who do not have the Spirit of Christ living in them do not belong to him at all.) And Christ lives within you, so even though your body will die because of sin, the Spirit gives you life because you have been made right with God. The Spirit of God, who raised Jesus from the dead, lives in you. And just as God raised Christ Jesus from the dead, he will give life to your mortal bodies by this same Spirit living within you. (Romans 8:9-11)

We know how much God loves us, and we have put our trust in his love. God is love, and all who live in love live in God, and God lives in them. And as we live in God, our love grows more perfect. So we will not be afraid on the day of judgment, but we can face him with confidence because we live like Jesus here in this world. Such love has no fear, because perfect love expels all fear. If we are afraid, it is for fear of punishment, and this shows that we have not fully experienced his perfect love. We love each other because he loved us first. (1 John 4:16-19)

For God has not given us a spirit of fear and timidity, but of power, love, and self-discipline. (2 Timothy 1:7)

He lifted me out of the pit of despair, out of the mud and the mire. He set my feet on solid ground and steadied me as I walked along. (Psalm 40:2)

But in my distress I cried out to the Lord; yes, I prayed to my God for help. He heard me from his sanctuary; my cry to him reached his ears. (Psalm 18:6)

And this same God who takes care of me will supply all your needs from his glorious riches, which have been given to us in Christ Jesus. (Philippians 4:19)

For the Lord God is our sun and our shield. He gives us grace and glory. The Lord will withhold no good thing from those who do what is right. (Psalm 84:11)

Your word is a lamp to guide my feet and a light for my path. (Psalm 119:105)

Work willingly at whatever you do, as though you were working for the Lord rather than for people. (Colossians 3:23)

Chapter 10: Encouragement

And we know that God causes everything to work together for the good of those who love God and are called according to his purpose for them. (Romans 8:28)

What shall we say about such wonderful things as these? If God is for us, who can ever be against us? (Romans 8:31)

He replied, "What is impossible for people is possible with God." (Luke 18:27)

...Here on earth you will have many trials and sorrows. But take heart, because I have overcome the world." (John 16:33)

So be strong and courageous! Do not be afraid and do not panic before them. For the Lord your God will personally go ahead of you. He will neither fail you nor abandon you." (Deuteronomy 31:6)

And I am certain that God, who began the good work within you, will continue his work until it is finally finished on the day when Christ Jesus returns. (Philippians 1:6)

The Spirit who lives in you is greater than the spirit who lives in the world. (1 John 4:4)

Come close to God, and God will come close to you... (James 4:8)

Have you never heard? Have you never understood? The Lord is the everlasting God, the Creator of all the earth. He never grows weak or weary. No one can measure the depths of his understanding. He gives power to the weak and strength to the powerless. Even youths will become weak and tired, and young men will fall in exhaustion. But those who trust in the Lord will find new strength. They will soar high on wings like eagles. They will run and not grow weary. They will walk and not faint. (Isaiah 40:28-31)

That is why we never give up. Though our bodies are dying, our spirits are being renewed every day. For our present troubles are small and won't last very long. Yet they produce for us a glory that vastly outweighs them and will last forever! So we don't look at the troubles we can see now; rather, we fix our gaze on things that cannot be seen. For the things we see now will soon be gone, but the things we cannot see will last forever. (2 Corinthians 4:16-18)

God is not a man, so he does not lie. He is not human, so he does not change his mind. Has he ever spoken and failed to act? Has he ever promised and not carried it through? (Numbers 23:19)

Give your burdens to the Lord, and he will take care of you. He will not permit the godly to slip and fall. (Psalm 55:22)

But if you remain in me and my words remain in you, you may ask for anything you want, and it will be granted! (John 15:7)

Chapter 11: Fear

Submit yourselves therefore to God. Resist the devil, and he will flee from you. (James 4:7)

So be strong and courageous, all you who put your hope in the Lord! (Psalm 31:24)

The Lord is for me, so I will have no fear. What can mere people do to me? (Psalm 118:6)

For the Lord your God is living among you. He is a mighty savior. He will take delight in you with gladness. With his love, he will calm all your fears. He will rejoice over you with joyful songs." (Zephaniah 3:17)

But you belong to God, my dear children. You have already won a victory over those people, because the Spirit who lives in you is greater than the spirit who lives in the world. (1 John 4:4)

Chapter 12: Finances

Good people leave an inheritance to their grandchildren, but the sinner's wealth passes to the godly. (Proverbs 13:22)

For the love of money is the root of all kinds of evil. And some people, craving money, have wandered from the true faith and pierced themselves with many sorrows. (1 Timothy 6:10)

No one can serve two masters. For you will hate one and love the other; you will be devoted to one and despise the other. You cannot serve both God and money. (Matthew 6:24)

Give to everyone what you owe them: Pay your taxes and government fees to those who collect them, and give respect and honor to those who are in authority. Owe nothing to anyone—except for your obligation to love one another. If you love your neighbor, you will fulfill the requirements of God's law. (Romans 13:7-8)

The wicked borrow and never repay, but the godly are generous givers. (Psalm 37:21)

With your wisdom and understanding you have amassed great wealth—gold and silver for your treasuries. (Ezekiel 28:4)

Chapter 13: Forgiveness

Don't repay evil for evil. Don't retaliate with insults when people insult you. Instead, pay them back with a blessing. That is what God has called you to do, and he will grant you his blessing. (1 Peter 3:9)

Do not judge others, and you will not be judged. Do not condemn others, or it will all come back against you. Forgive others, and you will be forgiven. (Luke 6:37)

God blesses those who are merciful, for they will be shown mercy. (Matthew 5:7)

Give us today the food we need, and forgive us our sins, as we have forgiven those who sin against us. And don't let us yield to temptation, but rescue us from the evil one. "If you forgive those who sin against you, your heavenly Father will forgive you. But if you refuse to forgive others, your Father will not forgive your sins. (Matthew 6:11-15)

Chapter 14: Guilt

Do not remember the rebellious sins of my youth. Remember me in the light of your unfailing love, for you are merciful, O Lord. (Psalm 25:7)

Though we are overwhelmed by our sins, you forgive them all. (Psalm 65:3)

How can I know all the sins lurking in my heart? Cleanse me from these hidden faults. Keep your servant from deliberate sins! Don't let them control me. Then I will be free of guilt and innocent of great sin. May the words of my mouth and the meditation of my heart be pleasing to you, O Lord, my rock and my redeemer. (Psalm 19:10-14)

I—yes, I alone—will blot out your sins for my own sake and will never think of them again. (Isaiah 43:25)

Oh, what joy for those whose disobedience is forgiven, whose sin is put out of sight! Yes, what joy for those whose record the Lord has cleared of guilt, whose lives are lived in complete honesty! (Psalm 32:1-2)

Chapter 15: Healing

But he was pierced for our rebellion, crushed for our sins. He was beaten so we could be whole. He was whipped so we could be healed. (Isaiah 53:5)

My child, pay attention to what I say. Listen carefully to my words. Don't lose sight of them. Let them penetrate deep into your heart, for they bring life to those who find them, and healing to their whole body. (Proverbs 4:20-22)

He sent out his word and healed them, snatching them from the door of death. (Psalm 107:20)

The Spirit of God, who raised Jesus from the dead, lives in you. And just as God raised Christ Jesus from the dead, he will give life to your mortal bodies by this same Spirit living within you. (Romans 8:11)

Chapter 16: Homework

For God has not given us a spirit of fear and timidity, but of power, love, and self-discipline. (2 Timothy 1:7)

"Who can know the LORD's thoughts? Who knows enough to teach him?" But we understand these things, for we have the mind of Christ. (1 Corinthians 2:16)

Work willingly at whatever you do, as though you were working for the Lord rather than for people. Remember that the Lord will give you an inheritance as your reward, and that the Master you are serving is Christ. (Colossians 3:23-24)

All Scripture is inspired by God and is useful to teach us what is true and to make us realize what is wrong in our lives. It corrects us when we are wrong and teaches us to do what is right. (2 Timothy 3:16)

Chapter 17: Hope

So be strong and courageous, all you who put your hope in the Lord! (Psalm 31:24)

Having hope will give you courage. You will be protected and will rest in safety. (Job 11:18)

Lead me by your truth and teach me, for you are the God who saves me. All day long I put my hope in you. (Psalm 25:5)

We put our hope in the LORD. He is our help and our shield. In him our hearts rejoice, for we trust in his holy name. Let your unfailing love surround us, LORD, for our hope is in you alone. (Psalm 33:20-21)

Let all that I am wait quietly before God, for my hope is in him. (Psalm 62:5)

Rejoice in our confident hope. Be patient in trouble, and keep on praying. (Romans 12:12)

I pray that your hearts will be flooded with light so that you can understand the confident hope he has given to those he called—his holy people who are his rich and glorious inheritance. (Ephesians 1:18)

And we know that God causes everything to work together for the good of those who love God and are called according to his purpose for them. (Romans 8:28)

You faithfully answer our prayers with awesome deeds, O God our savior. You are the hope of everyone on earth, even those who sail on distant seas. (Psalm 65:5)

But I will keep on hoping for your help; I will praise you more and more. (Psalm 71:14)

All praise to God, the Father of our Lord Jesus Christ. It is by his great mercy that we have been born again, because God raised Jesus Christ from the dead. Now we live with great expectation... (1 Peter 1:3)

Why am I discouraged? Why is my heart so sad? I will put my hope in God! I will praise him again— my Savior and my God! (Psalm 43:5)

Put your hope in the Lord. Travel steadily along his path. (Psalm 37:34)

"What do you mean, 'If I can'?" Jesus asked. "Anything is possible if a person believes." (Mark 9:23)

Chapter 18: Loneliness

"...be strong and courageous! Do not be afraid and do not panic before them. For the Lord your God will personally go ahead of you. He will neither fail you nor abandon you." (Deuteronomy 31:6)

Can anything ever separate us from Christ's love? Does it mean he no longer loves us if we have trouble or calamity, or are persecuted, or hungry, or destitute, or in danger, or threatened with death? ... No, despite all these things, overwhelming victory is ours through Christ, who loved us. (Romans 8:35,37)

Even if my father and mother abandon me, the Lord will hold me close. (Psalm 27:10)

Those who know your name trust in you, for you, O Lord, do not abandon those who search for you. (Psalm 9:10)

If you look for me wholeheartedly, you will find me. (Jeremiah 29:13)

Chapter 19: Marriage

Didn't the Lord make you one with your wife? In body and spirit you are his. And what does he want? Godly children from your union. So guard your heart; remain loyal to the wife of your youth. (Malachi 2:15)

Let your wife be a fountain of blessing for you. Rejoice in the wife of your youth. (Proverbs 5:18)

So God created human beings in his own image. In the image of God he created them; male and female he created them. Then God blessed them and said, "Be fruitful and multiply..." (Genesis 1:27-28)

Fathers can give their sons an inheritance of houses and wealth, but only the Lord can give an understanding wife. (Proverbs 19:14)

In the same way, you husbands must give honor to your wives. Treat your wife with understanding as you live together. She may be weaker than you are, but she is your equal partner in God's gift of new life. Treat her as you should so your prayers will not be hindered. (1 Peter 3:7)

Who can find a virtuous and capable wife? She is more precious than rubies. Her husband can trust her, and she will greatly enrich his life. She brings him good, not harm, all the days of her life. (Proverbs 31:10-12)

And further, submit to one another out of reverence for Christ. For wives, this means submit to your husbands as to the Lord. For a husband is the head of his wife as Christ is the head of the church. He is the Savior of his body, the church. As the church submits to Christ, so you wives should submit to your husbands in everything. For husbands, this means love your wives, just as Christ loved the church. He gave up his life for her to make her holy and clean, washed by the cleansing of God's word. He did this to present her to himself as a glorious church without a spot or wrinkle or any other blemish. Instead, she will be holy and without fault. In the same way, husbands ought to love their wives as they love their own bodies. For a man who loves his wife actually shows love for himself. No one hates his own body but feeds and cares for it, just as Christ cares for the church. And we are members of his body. As the Scriptures say, "A man leaves his father and mother and is joined to his wife, and the two are united into one." This is a great mystery, but it is an illustration of the way Christ and the church are one. So again I say, each man must love his wife as he loves himself, and the wife must respect her husband. (Ephesians 5:21-33)

Chapter 20: Overwhelmed

From the ends of the earth, I cry to you for help when my heart is overwhelmed. Lead me to the towering rock of safety, for you are my safe refuge, a fortress where my enemies cannot reach me. (Psalm 61:2-3)

So you see, the Lord knows how to rescue godly people from their trials... (2 Peter 2:9)

But in my distress I cried out to the Lord; yes, I prayed to my God for help. He heard me from his sanctuary; my cry to him reached his ears. (Psalm 18:6)

I look up to the mountains— does my help come from there? My help comes from the Lord, who made heaven and earth! (Psalm 121:1-2)

Don't let your hearts be troubled. Trust in God, and trust also in me. (John 14:1)

Then call on me when you are in trouble, and I will rescue you, and you will give me glory." (Psalm 50:15)

Don't be afraid, for I am with you. Don't be discouraged, for I am your God. I will strengthen you and help you. I will hold you up with my victorious right hand. (Isaiah 41:10)

When you go through deep waters, I will be with you. When you go through rivers of difficulty, you will not drown. When you walk through the fire of oppression, you will not be burned up; the flames will not consume you. (Isaiah 43:2)

"I am the Lord, the God of all the peoples of the world. Is anything too hard for me? (Jeremiah 32:27)

Jesus looked at them intently and said, "Humanly speaking, it is impossible. But with God everything is possible." (Matthew 19:26)

I have told you all this so that you may have peace in me. Here on earth you will have many trials and sorrows. But take heart, because I have overcome the world." (John 16:33)

But those who trust in the Lord will find new strength. They will soar high on wings like eagles. They will run and not grow weary. They will walk and not faint. (Isaiah 40:31)

For our present troubles are small and won't last very long. Yet they produce for us a glory that vastly outweighs them and will last forever! (2 Corinthians 4:17)

I pray that God, the source of hope, will fill you completely with joy and peace because you trust in him. Then you will overflow with confident hope through the power of the Holy Spirit. (Romans 15:13)

Chapter 21: Parents

Listen to your father, who gave you life, and don't despise your mother when she is old. (Proverbs 23:22)

Fathers, do not provoke your children to anger by the way you treat them. Rather, bring them up with the discipline and instruction that comes from the Lord. (Ephesians 6:4)

My son, obey your father's commands, and don't neglect your mother's instruction. (Proverbs 6:20)

Honor your father and mother. Love your neighbor as yourself. (Matthew 19:19)

Chapter 22: Patience

A servant of the Lord must not quarrel but must be kind to everyone, be able to teach, and be patient with difficult people. (2 Timothy 2:24)

Be still in the presence of the Lord, and wait patiently for him to act. (Psalm 37:7)

Let all that I am wait quietly before God, for my hope is in him. He alone is my rock and my salvation, my fortress where I will not be shaken. My victory and honor come from God alone. He is my refuge, a rock where no enemy can reach me. (Psalm 62:5-7)

And the seeds that fell on the good soil represent honest, good-hearted people who hear God's word, cling to it, and patiently produce a huge harvest. (Luke 8:15)

Such things were written in the Scriptures long ago to teach us. And the Scriptures give us hope and encouragement as we wait patiently for God's promises to be fulfilled. May God, who gives this patience and encouragement, help you live in complete harmony with each other, as is fitting for followers of Christ Jesus. (Romans 15:4-5)

Chapter 23: Peace

So letting your sinful nature control your mind leads to death. But letting the Spirit control your mind leads to life and peace. (Romans 8:6)

Above all, clothe yourselves with love, which binds us all together in perfect harmony. And let the peace that comes from Christ rule in your hearts. For as members of one body you are called to live in peace. And always be thankful. (Colossians 3:14-15)

"I have told you all this so that you may have peace in me. Here on earth you will have many trials and sorrows. But take heart, because I have overcome the world." (John 16:33)

Therefore, since we have been made right in God's sight by faith, we have peace with God because of what Jesus Christ our Lord has done for us. (Romans 5:1)

And now may God, who gives us his peace, be with you all. Amen. (Romans 15:33)

God blesses those who work for peace, for they will be called the children of God. (Matthew 5:9)

You will keep in perfect peace all who trust in you, all whose thoughts are fixed on you! Trust in the Lord always, for the Lord God is the eternal Rock. (Isaiah 26:3-4)

Chapter 24: Perseverance

But if you remain in me and my words remain in you, you may ask for anything you want, and it will be granted! (John 15:7)

I have told you all this so that you may have peace in me. Here on earth you will have many trials and sorrows. But take heart, because I have overcome the world." (John 16:33)

Rejoice in our confident hope. Be patient in trouble, and keep on praying. (Romans 12:12)

So, my dear brothers and sisters, be strong and immovable. Always work enthusiastically for the Lord, for you know that nothing you do for the Lord is ever useless. (1 Corinthians 15:58)

Be on guard. Stand firm in the faith. Be courageous. Be strong. And do everything with love. (1 Corinthians 16:13-14)

He replied, "What is impossible for people is possible with God."
(Luke 18:27)

So let's not get tired of doing what is good. At just the right time we
will reap a harvest of blessing if we don't give up. Therefore, whenever we have the opportunity, we should do good to everyone—
especially to those in the family of faith. (Galatians 6:9-10)

And I am certain that God, who began the good work within you, will
continue his work until it is finally finished on the day when Christ
Jesus returns. (Philippians 1:6)

For if we are faithful to the end, trusting God just as firmly as
when we first believed, we will share in all that belongs to Christ.
(Hebrews 3:14)

Let us hold tightly without wavering to the hope we affirm, for God
can be trusted to keep his promise. (Hebrews 10:23)

We can rejoice, too, when we run into problems and trials, for we
know that they help us develop endurance. And endurance develops
strength of character, and character strengthens our confident hope
of salvation. (Romans 5:3-4)

That is why we never give up. Though our bodies are dying, our
spirits are being renewed every day. For our present troubles are
small and won't last very long. Yet they produce for us a glory that
vastly outweighs them and will last forever! So we don't look at
the troubles we can see now; rather, we fix our gaze on things that
cannot be seen. For the things we see now will soon be gone, but
the things we cannot see will last forever. (2 Corinthians 4:16-18)

Chapter 25: Pornography

Run from sexual sin! No other sin so clearly affects the body as this one does. For sexual immorality is a sin against your own body. Don't you realize that your body is the temple of the Holy Spirit, who lives in you and was given to you by God? You do not belong to yourself, for God bought you with a high price. So you must honor God with your body. (1 Corinthians 6:18-20)

Don't you realize that those who do wrong will not inherit the Kingdom of God? Don't fool yourselves. Those who indulge in sexual sin, or who worship idols, or commit adultery, or are male prostitutes, or practice homosexuality... (1 Corinthians 6:9)

You say, "Food was made for the stomach, and the stomach for food." (This is true, though someday God will do away with both of them.) But you can't say that our bodies were made for sexual immorality. They were made for the Lord, and the Lord cares about our bodies. (1 Corinthians 6:13)

...keep away from worldly desires that wage war against your very souls. (1 Peter 2:11)

Chapter 26: Pregnancy

So be strong and courageous! Do not be afraid and do not panic before them. For the Lord your God will personally go ahead of you. He will neither fail you nor abandon you." (Deuteronomy 31:6)

Give your burdens to the Lord, and he will take care of you. He will not permit the godly to slip and fall. (Psalm 55:22)

I was thrust into your arms at my birth. You have been my God from the moment I was born. (Psalms 22:10)

Give all your worries and cares to God, for he cares about you. (1 Peter 5:7)

Chapter 27: Protection

Let all that I am wait quietly before God, for my hope is in him. He alone is my rock and my salvation, my fortress where I will not be shaken. My victory and honor come from God alone. He is my refuge, a rock where no enemy can reach me. (Psalm 62:5-7)

In peace I will lie down and sleep, for you alone, O Lord, will keep me safe. (Psalm 4:8)

I wait quietly before God, for my victory comes from him. He alone is my rock and my salvation, my fortress where I will never be shaken. (Psalm 62:1-2)

The Lord is a shelter for the oppressed, a refuge in times of trouble. (Psalm 9:9)

Those who live in the shelter of the Most High will find rest in the shadow of the Almighty. This I declare about the Lord: He alone is my refuge, my place of safety; he is my God, and I trust him. (Psalm 91:1-2)

I look up to the mountains—does my help come from there? My help comes from the Lord,

who made heaven and earth! He will not let you stumble; the one who watches over you will not slumber. Indeed, he who watches over Israel never slumbers or sleeps. The Lord himself watches over you! The Lord stands beside you as your protective shade. The sun will not harm you by day, nor the moon at night. The Lord keeps you from all harm and watches over your life. The Lord keeps watch over you as you come and go, both now and forever. (Psalm 121:1-8)

God is our refuge and strength, always ready to help in times of trouble. (Psalm 46:1)

For the Lord loves justice, and he will never abandon the godly. He will keep them safe forever... (Psalm 37:28)

Though I am surrounded by troubles, you will protect me from the anger of my enemies. You reach out your hand, and the power of your right hand saves me. (Psalm 138:7)

Rescue me from my enemies, O God. Protect me from those who have come to destroy me. (Psalm 59:1)

My enemies will retreat when I call to you for help. This I know: God is on my side! (Psalm 56:9)

I'm not asking you to take them out of the world, but to keep them safe from the evil one. (John 17:15)

We know that God's children do not make a practice of sinning, for God's Son holds them securely, and the evil one cannot touch them. (1 John 5:18)

The eternal God is your refuge, and his everlasting arms are under you. (Deuteronomy 33:27)

Chapter 28: Rest

For I have given rest to the weary and joy to the sorrowing."
(Jeremiah 31:25)

This is what the Lord says: "Stop at the crossroads and look around. Ask for the old, godly way, and walk in it. Travel its path, and you will find rest for your souls. (Jeremiah 6:16)

It is useless for you to work so hard from early morning until late at night, anxiously working for food to eat; for God gives rest to his loved ones. (Psalm 127: 2)

Chapter 29: Salvation

Jew and Gentile are the same in this respect. They have the same Lord, who gives generously to all who call on him. For "Everyone who calls on the name of the Lord will be saved." (Romans 10:12-13)

But—When God our Savior revealed his kindness and love, he saved us, not because of the righteous things we had done, but because of his mercy. He washed away our sins, giving us a new birth and new life through the Holy Spirit. (Titus 3:4-5)

This means that anyone who belongs to Christ has become a new person. The old life is gone; a new life has begun! (2 Corinthians 5:17)

Don't copy the behavior and customs of this world, but let God transform you into a new person by changing the way you think. Then you will learn to know God's will for you, which is good and pleasing and perfect. (Romans 12:2)

For once you were full of darkness, but now you have light from the Lord. So live as people of light! (Ephesians 5:8)

Therefore, since we have been made right in God's sight by faith, we have peace with God because of what Jesus Christ our Lord has done for us. (Romans 5:1)

Yet we know that a person is made right with God by faith in Jesus Christ, not by obeying the law. And we have believed in Christ Jesus, so that we might be made right with God because of our faith in Christ, not because we have obeyed the law. For no one will ever be made right with God by obeying the law." (Galatians 2:16)

And since it is through God's kindness, then it is not by their good works. For in that case, God's grace would not be what it really is— free and undeserved. (Romans 11:6)

Those who accept my commandments and obey them are the ones who love me. And because they love me, my Father will love them. And I will love them and reveal myself to each of them." Jesus replied, "All who love me will do what I say. My Father will love them, and we will come and make our home with each of them. (John 14:21, 23)

He personally carried our sins in his body on the cross so that we can be dead to sin and live for what is right. By his wounds you are healed. (1 Peter 2:24)

O Lord, if you heal me, I will be truly healed; if you save me, I will be truly saved. My praises are for you alone! (Jeremiah 17:14)

He will wipe every tear from their eyes, and there will be no more death or sorrow or crying or pain. All these things are gone forever. (Revelation 21:3-4)

I give them eternal life, and they will never perish. No one can snatch them away from me, for my Father has given them to me, and he is more powerful than anyone else. No one can snatch them from the Father's hand. (John 10:28-29)

Chapter 30: Self-esteem

"For this is how God loved the world: He gave his one and only Son, so that everyone who believes in him will not perish but have eternal life. (John 3:16)

See how very much our Father loves us, for he calls us his children, and that is what we are! But the people who belong to this world don't recognize that we are God's children because they don't know him. (1 John 3:1)

But to all who believed him and accepted him, he gave the right to become children of God. (John 1:12)

This means that anyone who belongs to Christ has become a new person. The old life is gone; a new life has begun! (2 Corinthians 5:17)

I am in them and you are in me. May they experience such perfect unity that the world will know that you sent me and that you love them as much as you love me. (John 17:23)

It is better to take refuge in the Lord than to trust in people. (Psalm 118:8)

Those who accept my commandments and obey them are the ones who love me. And because they love me, my Father will love them. And I will love them and reveal myself to each of them." (John 14:21)

Chapter 31: Sex

Young people who obey the law are wise; those with wild friends bring shame to their parents. (Proverbs 28:7)

Give honor to marriage, and remain faithful to one another in marriage. God will surely judge people who are immoral and those who commit adultery. (Hebrews 13:4)

For the world offers only a craving for physical pleasure, a craving for everything we see, and pride in our achievements and posses-sions. These are not from the Father, but are from this world. (1 John 2:16)

This explains why a man leaves his father and mother and is joined to his wife, and the two are united into one. (Genesis 2:24)

But because there is so much sexual immorality, each man should have his own wife, and each woman should have her own husband. The husband should fulfill his wife's sexual needs, and the wife should fulfill her husband's needs. The wife gives authority over her body to her husband, and the husband gives authority over his body to his wife. (1 Corinthians 7:2-4)

Chapter 32: Suicide

For "Everyone who calls on the name of the Lord will be saved." (Romans 10:13)

The thief's purpose is to steal and kill and destroy. My purpose is to give them a rich and satisfying life. (John 10:10)

Don't copy the behavior and customs of this world, but let God trans-form you into a new person by changing the way you think. Then you will learn to know God's will for you, which is good and pleasing and perfect. (Romans 12:2)

We are pressed on every side by troubles, but we are not crushed. We are perplexed, but not driven to despair. We are hunted down, but never abandoned by God. We get knocked down, but we are not destroyed. (2 Corinthians 4:8-9)

How long must I struggle with anguish in my soul, with sorrow in my heart every day? How long will my enemy have the upper hand? Turn and answer me, O Lord my God! Restore the sparkle to my eyes, or I will die. (Psalm 13:2-3)

Chapter 33: Temptation

I am warning you ahead of time, dear friends. Be on guard so that you will not be carried away by the errors of these wicked people and lose your own secure footing. Rather, you must grow in the grace and knowledge of our Lord and Savior Jesus Christ. All glory to him, both now and forever! Amen. (2 Peter 3:17-18)

You say, "I am allowed to do anything"—but not everything is good for you. You say, "I am allowed to do anything"—but not everything is beneficial. (1 Corinthians 10:23)

But people who long to be rich fall into temptation and are trapped by many foolish and harmful desires that plunge them into ruin and destruction. (1 Timothy 6:9)

Chapter 34: Your Future

And we will receive from him whatever we ask because we obey him and do the things that please him. (1 John 3:22)

"So don't worry about these things, saying, 'What will we eat? What will we drink? What will we wear?' These things dominate the thoughts of unbelievers, but your heavenly Father already knows all your needs. Seek the Kingdom of God[a] above all else, and live righteously, and he will give you everything you need. (Matthew 6:31-33)

And I am certain that God, who began the good work within you, will continue his work until it is finally finished on the day when Christ Jesus returns. (Philippians 1:6)

For we are God's masterpiece. He has created us anew in Christ Jesus, so we can do the good things he planned for us long ago. (Ephesians 2:10)

Look at those who are honest and good, for a wonderful future awaits those who love peace. (Psalm 37:37)

My thoughts are nothing like your thoughts," says the Lord. "And my ways are far beyond anything you could imagine. For just as the heavens are higher than the earth, so my ways are higher than your ways and my thoughts higher than your thoughts. (Isaiah 55:8-9)

You can make many plans, but the Lord's purpose will prevail. (Proverbs 19:21)

And we know that God causes everything to work together for the good of those who love God and are called according to his purpose for them. (Romans 8:28)

My child, never forget the things I have taught you. Store my commands in your heart. If you do this, you will live many years, and your life will be satisfying. Never let loyalty and kindness leave you! Tie them around your neck as a reminder. Write them deep within your heart. Then you will find favor with both God and people, and you will earn a good reputation. (Proverbs 3:1-4)

Chapter 35: Wisdom

Fear of the Lord is the foundation of true wisdom. All who obey his commandments will grow in wisdom. (Psalm 111:10)

My children, listen when your father corrects you. Pay attention and learn good judgment, for I am giving you good guidance. Don't turn away from my instructions. For I, too, was once my father's son, tenderly loved as my mother's only child. My father taught me, "Take my words to heart. Follow my commands, and you will live. Get wisdom; develop good judgment. Don't forget my words or turn away from them. Don't turn your back on wisdom, for she will protect you. Love her, and she will guard you. Getting wisdom is the wisest thing you can do! And whatever else you do, develop good judgment. If you prize wisdom, she will make you great. Embrace her, and she will honor you. She will place a lovely wreath on your head; she will present you with a beautiful crown." My child, listen to me and do as I say, and you will have a long, good life. I will teach you wisdom's ways and lead you in straight paths. When you walk, you won't be held back; when you run, you won't stumble. Take hold of my instructions; don't let them go. Guard them, for they are the key to life. (Proverbs 4:1-13)

The instruction of the wise is like a life-giving fountain; those who accept it avoid the snares of death. (Proverbs 13:14)

The wise are cautious and avoid danger; fools plunge ahead with reckless confidence. (Proverbs 14:16)

The lips of the wise give good advice; the heart of a fool has none to give. (Proverbs 15:7)

If you reject discipline, you only harm yourself; but if you listen to correction, you grow in understanding. Fear of the Lord teaches wisdom; humility precedes honor. (Proverbs 15:32-33)

Those who listen to instruction will prosper; those who trust the Lord will be joyful. The wise are known for their understanding, and pleasant words are persuasive. (Proverbs 16:20-21)

Intelligent people are always ready to learn. Their ears are open for knowledge. (Proverbs 18:15)

To acquire wisdom is to love oneself; people who cherish understanding will prosper.(Proverbs 19:8)

Commit yourself to instruction; listen carefully to words of knowledge. (Proverbs 23:12)

How wonderful to be wise, to analyze and interpret things. Wisdom lights up a person's face, softening its harshness. (Ecclesiastes 8:1)

"Anyone who listens to my teaching and follows it is wise, like a person who builds a house on solid rock. (Matthew 7:24)

If you are wise and understand God's ways, prove it by living an honorable life, doing good works with the humility that comes from wisdom. (James 3:13)

CPSIA information can be obtained
at www.ICGtesting.com
Printed in the USA
FSOW02n1648020517
33794FS